National Trust

COMFORT FOOD

National Trust

COMFORT FOOD

RECIPES BY
Clive Goudercourt &
The National Trust Cafés

National Trust

First published in the United Kingdom in 2019 by
National Trust Books
43 Great Ormond Street
London WC1N 3HZ

An imprint of Pavilion Books Company Ltd

ISBN: 9781911358541

A CIP catalogue record for this book is available from the British Library.

10 9 8 7 6 5 4 3 2 1

Reproduction by Misson Productions, Hong Kong
Printed by 1010 Printing International Ltd, China

Project Consultant: Sara Lewis
Photographer: Nassima Rothacker
Home Economist: Annie Rigg
Prop Stylist: Tabitha Hawkins
Creative Director: Helen Lewis
Senior Commissioning Editor: Peter Taylor
Senior Editor: Lucy Smith
Senior Designer: Gemma Doyle

With thanks to The National Trust Food & Beverage Team, particularly Tim Howard and
Julie Comer, and to Maria Aversa and India Whiley-Morton for their help on the photoshoot.

This book can be ordered direct from the publisher at the website
www.pavilionbooks.com, or try your local bookshop.
Also available at National Trust shops or www.shop.nationaltrust.org.uk

MIX
Paper from
responsible sources
FSC® C016973

Contents

There's never a mundane day when your job involves making dishes from scratch. Especially when you work for a charity that serves up 2 million scones and 14 million cups of tea every year. Since we published the first *National Trust Cookbook* in 2016, I've also been lucky enough to try cooking on a coal-fired range in Northern Ireland and even made a five-foot replica of Souter Lighthouse, Tyne & Wear, from cake.

Back to the day-to-day and, in my role as the Trust's Development Chef, I've been busy putting together lots more seasonal recipes to be enjoyed in our – almost – 350 cafés. This new *National Trust Comfort Food* cookbook shares some of the most heartening. There are the dishes perfect for ladling into a bowl to accompany an evening on the sofa after a tough day at work, or for munching while lounging on a blanket in the garden or local park (or the grounds of your favourite Trust property) alongside friends, family or a good book.

I find there's something very comforting, and satisfying, about eating ingredients that are local and in season too. It's so rewarding to pick a vegetable or herb from the garden, allotment or window box and see it on your plate an hour later. The seasonality of ingredients, and where they have come from, are also incredibly important to us as a conservation charity. So, although some of my inspiration comes from the wider world and trends, it is these two things that are always at the very forefront of my mind. As a result, our café dishes change throughout the year, and we've reflected this by dividing up the recipes in this book by season. This also means it's easy to find the perfect dish to suit the weather – and to help you use up gluts of home-grown fruit and veg.

Hazy, lazy summer days inspired the Picnic Pie and Relish on page 73, which is perfect for taking out on adventures with family and friends. (My personal favourite spot to enjoy it? Clumber Park in Nottinghamshire. It's the place I started my journey with the National Trust and you'll often find me back there, cycling in the

grounds or taking in the historic rhubarb collection in the Walled Garden.) As the temperature cools, I turn to warmer dishes: the Fragrant Leek and Sweet Potato Soup on page 152 is best served after a winter walk, when chilly winds have made your cheeks pink and somehow permeated even the warmest of gloves. I'll let you into a secret: this is also my favourite recipe in the whole of this new cookbook. It's so simple but when you add the green part of the leek back into the soup, it ends up with amazing, vibrant, green-coloured flecks which still have a little crunch in them, and the flavours pack a proper punch. It's a real comfort dish.

Talking of flavours, you'll also find a wider range in this cookbook than the last one. Even in the past few years, tastes have changed as people travel more and further around the globe, and it's become easier to get hold of exotic ingredients too. I've tried to reflect this in our café dishes, which include the refreshing Vietnamese Chicken Salad on page 71 and the flavourful meat-free Vegetable and Coconut Curry on page 39.

But even with a world of flavours to play with, it's often the most simple places, close to home, that provide the best inspiration – just picking a strawberry fresh from a National Trust kitchen garden, giving it a quick rinse and then dipping it into rich double cream lightly flavoured with vanilla, sprinkling over a few flakes of cracked black pepper and popping it into my mouth. Divine.

Often, my trips to National Trust places are whistle-stop tours. It is easy to just visit the car park and kitchens. But that's not what makes the National Trust, or our food. For me, it is the stories of the people who lived and worked there in times gone past that bring a place to life. Old documents from the kitchen can tell fascinating stories, too – of startling uses of unexpected ingredients and the extravagance the house would go to when entertaining. Some of them would have herbs and spices that might have cost the equivalent of a year's wages back then – imagine having all your herbs and spices locked away and only being accessed when the chef needed them. Or paying thousands of pounds for a cinnamon stick!

And of course the kitchen teams who work in these places today are also a huge wealth of inspiration. They have so many engaging ideas and it's exciting to see how they look at local ingredients and use them to enhance a recipe. There are some fantastic creations out there to try and we've picked several mouthwatering ones to give you a taste (pun intended) of their creativity. One can be found at Powis Castle, Powys, which was once home to Robert Clive of the East India Company. Among the many things he imported to the United Kingdom was quinine, an essential ingredient in tonic. His story led the café team to create their twist on a lemon drizzle: the Gin & Tonic Cake on page 50. Over in Cumbria, the Sticklebarn pub created a Lamb and Hawkshead Red Ale Stew (page 118), which celebrates two Lake District ingredients: Hawkshead Red, brewed in a tiny brewery with just five brewers; and delicious Herdwick lamb, which was famously farmed and championed by Beatrix Potter, who left 1,620 hectares (4,000 acres) of countryside, 14 farms and her house, Hill Top, to the National Trust.

Much as I love my job, it doesn't always go smoothly – even when making recipes I've made time and time again. I'll never forget my fruit scones disaster, especially because it happened in front of a live audience. I made the scones as usual, then cut and placed them on the tray. I put them in the oven and waited for them to cook and went on to talk about jam and cream. But they didn't rise. It turned out the flours had been switched and I'd used plain instead of self-raising. To make matters worse, the audience were all eagerly awaiting a promised taste of our most famous dish. After a hurried explanation of what had happened, I bid a hasty retreat to the back of the cookery theatre! It just goes to show that even professionals can have a bad day in the kitchen – so don't worry if not every recipe you try works perfectly first time (at least it's not being witnessed by 100 other people…).

After all, cooking should be enjoyable – as comforting to put together as the end result is to eat. I hope you enjoy making and eating our recipes as much as I enjoyed creating them.

Clive Goudercourt

Development Chef, National Trust

Spring

As the gardens and woodlands begin to awaken, so splashes of colour start to appear, with the first tiny snowdrops then dainty primroses and bright yellow daffodils, followed by carpets of bluebells and cloud-like bursts of apple and cherry blossom. As the days begin to lengthen you may begin to crave something a little lighter for supper. Try Goat's Cheese & Beetroot Oatcake, Curried Squash Tarts or Carrot, Cauliflower, Kale & Pomegranate Tabbouleh. For those colder days, try Sausage Bubble & Squeak with red wine and onion gravy finished off with early baby pink Rhubarb Shortbread with ginger cream, or steamed St Clement's Sponge.

Leek & potato soup

Tinged a delicate green, this timeless classic is given a modern twist with a drizzle of sage-flavoured rapeseed oil.

Serves 4–6
Prep 20 minutes
Cook 21–23 minutes

600g/1lb 6oz leeks, trimmed
1 tbsp vegetable oil
400g/14oz potatoes, peeled
  and cut into chunks
850ml/1½pt vegetable stock
Salt and pepper

TO FINISH
2 tbsp extra virgin rapeseed oil
1 tbsp fresh finely chopped
  sage

Slit the leeks lengthways with a knife, then wash well and drain. Thinly slice the top green half from each leek, put in a bowl and set aside. Thinly slice the remaining white leek.

Heat the oil in a large saucepan, add the white sliced leeks and fry for 2–3 minutes until just beginning to soften. Stir in the potatoes, half the stock and a little salt and pepper and bring to the boil. Cover and simmer for 15 minutes until the potatoes are soft.

Meanwhile add the rapeseed oil and sage to a small saucepan, heat gently until sizzling, then set aside and leave to cool.

Stir the reserved green sliced leeks and remaining stock into the soup pan, simmer for 2–3 minutes or until the leeks are soft but still bright green.

Purée the soup in the pan with a stick blender or transfer to a liquidiser, blend until smooth, then return to the pan. Taste and adjust the seasoning and reheat the soup if needed.

Ladle into bowls, drizzle with the sage oil and serve with bread and butter.

COOK'S TIP Don't be tempted to cook the soup for longer when adding the green leek tops or the soup will lose its lovely green colour.

Cream of chicken & tarragon soup

The creaminess of this soup combined with the freshness of the tarragon makes this a perfect combination for the drizzly days of early spring, when you long for something lighter but still feel a bit chilly.

Serves 4–6
Prep 20 minutes
Cook 30 minutes

1 tbsp vegetable oil
225g/8oz onion, finely chopped
70g/2½oz celery, finely chopped
2 boneless, skinless chicken thighs, about 150g/5½oz, diced
70g/2½oz leeks, finely chopped
70g/2½oz carrot, finely chopped
850ml/1½pt chicken stock
1 tbsp fresh finely chopped tarragon
Salt and pepper
2 tbsp cornflour
6 tbsp milk
4 tbsp double cream
Little extra chopped tarragon to garnish, optional

Heat the oil in a saucepan, add the onion and celery and fry over a medium heat for 5 minutes, stirring from time to time until softened.

Add the diced chicken and fry for 5 minutes, stirring until lightly browned. Mix in the leeks and carrots and stir well.

Pour in the stock, add the tarragon, season with a little salt and pepper and bring to the boil, then cover and simmer for 15 minutes until the chicken is tender.

Add the cornflour to a small bowl and mix to a smooth paste with half the milk. Pour into the saucepan with the remaining milk, bring back to the boil, then simmer for 5 minutes, stirring until thickened.

Stir in the cream, then taste and adjust the seasoning if needed. Ladle into bowls, sprinkle with a little extra chopped tarragon if liked and serve with warm bread and butter.

COOK'S TIP Tarragon adds a lovely flavour to soups and sauces but it has a much stronger taste than some other herbs, so use sparingly as a little goes a long way.

Carrot, spring onion & poppy seed soup

While the garden may be beginning to green up a little and the days getting longer, the temperature can still be a little unpredictable. Take the edge off the chillier days with this warming soup made from ingredients already in the kitchen.

Serves 4–6
Prep 20 minutes
Cook 45–50 minutes

700g/1lb 9oz carrots, scrubbed
  and roughly chopped
1 tbsp vegetable oil
200g/7oz onion, roughly
  chopped
100g/3 ½ oz potatoes, diced
2 garlic cloves, finely chopped
½ tsp dried sage
1 tsp dried mixed herbs
1.2ltr/2pt vegetable stock
2 tsp caster sugar
Salt and pepper

TO GARNISH
2 tbsp extra virgin rapeseed oil
2 spring onions, finely
  chopped
1 tsp poppy seeds

Preheat the oven to 180°C/350°F/gas mark 4. Add the carrots to a roasting tin, then bake in the oven for 30 minutes until lightly coloured.

Meanwhile, heat the oil in a saucepan, add the onion, potato and garlic and fry over a medium heat for 5 minutes, stirring from time to time without colouring. Mix in the sage and mixed herbs, cover with a lid and fry for a further 10 minutes, stirring from time to time until the potatoes have softened.

Stir the carrots into the pan with the onions and potato, then add the stock, sugar and a little salt and pepper. Bring to the boil, cover and simmer for 15–20 minutes until the vegetables are soft.

To make the garnish, heat the oil in a small frying pan, add the spring onions and poppy seeds, stir well then leave to cool. Cover and set aside.

Purée the soup in the pan with a stick blender or transfer to a liquidiser. Adjust with a little extra stock and salt and pepper, if needed. Reheat and ladle into bowls. Top with a drizzle of the spring onion and poppy seed oil.

Smoked mackerel Scotch eggs

Scotch eggs wrapped in sausagemeat are a pub classic – here the eggs are wrapped in a horseradish, parsley and potato mix speckled with smoked mackerel. Serve warm for supper or add to a lunchbox for a very special picnic addition.

Makes 4
Prep 30 minutes
Chill 30 minutes
Cook 10–12 minutes

4 eggs
115g/4oz smoked mackerel, skinned
250g/9oz cooked mashed potato
25g/1oz fresh breadcrumbs
4 tbsp fresh chopped parsley
15g/½oz fresh horseradish, peeled, grated
½ lemon, grated zest and juice
Salt and pepper

TO FINISH
2 tbsp plain flour
1 egg, beaten
60g/2¼oz fresh breadcrumbs
100ml/3½fl oz vegetable oil

Add the eggs to a saucepan of water, bring to the boil, then simmer for 6 minutes. Drain, crack the shells slightly and put the eggs back into cold water, before peeling away the shells. Set eggs aside on a plate.

Flake the mackerel into small pieces with two forks, then add to a bowl with the potato, breadcrumbs, parsley, horseradish, lemon zest and juice and a little salt and pepper. Mix well.

Divide the potato mixture into four. Flatten one quarter of the mixture in the palm of your hand and place an egg on top. Gently press the mixture around the egg to cover completely, then pat the potato mixture into an even thickness. Put back on the plate, cover with clingfilm and chill in the fridge for 30 minutes.

Preheat the oven to 180°C/350°F/gas mark 4. Put the flour on a saucer, the egg in a cereal bowl and the breadcrumbs on a plate. Roll each egg first in the flour, then coat in the egg and then the breadcrumbs until completely covered.

Heat the oil in a deep frying pan, add the eggs and fry for 2-3 minutes, gently rolling them in the hot oil with two forks, until lightly coloured and crisp all over. Lift the eggs out of the oil with a slotted spoon and transfer to a roasting tin. Bake in the oven for 2–3 minutes until browned. Leave to cool on kitchen towel, then cut in half and serve with salad and a little mayonnaise.

COOK'S TIP This recipe is a good way to use up leftover mashed potato or the soft centres from baked potatoes.

Make sure to taste the potato mixture before shaping around the eggs to check on the seasoning.

Tuscan bean soup

If you've had a bad day at work then this warming bowl of goodness will help reduce the stress of the day, especially if eaten on a comfy sofa with something good on the television.

Serves 4–6
Prep 15 minutes
Cook 23 minutes

1 tbsp vegetable oil
100g/3½oz onions, finely chopped
1 garlic clove, finely chopped
140g/5oz carrots, finely diced
2 sticks celery, finely diced
100g/3½oz cauliflower florets, finely chopped
2 tbsp tomato purée
340g/12oz tomatoes, chopped
600ml/1pt vegetable stock
10g/¼oz fresh parsley, chopped
1x 400g/14oz can 5-bean mix or mixed pulses in water, drained
2 spring onions, finely chopped
Salt and pepper

Heat the oil in a saucepan, add the onion, garlic, carrots, celery and cauliflower and fry over a medium heat for 10 minutes, stirring from time to time until softened.

Stir in the tomato purée and cook for 3 minutes, then mix in the fresh tomatoes, stock and half the parsley. Bring to the boil, then cover and simmer for 5 minutes.

Mix in the remaining parsley, canned beans and spring onions. Season to taste, then simmer for 5 minutes.

Ladle the hot soup into bowls and serve with a hunk of bread.

COOK'S TIP This tastes delicious sprinkled with a little grated smoked cheddar or parmesan.

Why not eat half the soup and freeze the other two portions in individual plastic containers – they make a great standby supper to defrost in the microwave.

Kids' chicken noodle soup

Turn the leftovers from yesterday's roast chicken into this gently spiced, clear chicken soup. If you have time, simmer the carcass earlier in the day or the night before with water, a diced onion, carrot, leek top and a few herbs for 1½ hours to make a delicious homemade stock for the soup.

Serves 4
Prep 15 minutes
Cook 8 minutes

50g/1¾oz mangetout, sliced
50g/1¾oz sprouting broccoli, thinly sliced
50g/1¾oz frozen peas
50g/1¾oz frozen sweetcorn
60g/2¼oz red pepper, cored, deseeded, thinly sliced
100g/3½oz beansprouts, rinsed well in cold water then drained
85g/3oz fine rice noodles, cooked as pack instructions
200g/7oz cooked chicken, torn into small shreds

FOR THE BROTH
850ml/1½pt chicken stock
½ tsp ground coriander
½ tsp ground ginger
3 small star anise
1 tbsp soya sauce
Salt and pepper
2 tbsp fresh chopped coriander

Add the mangetout, broccoli, peas and sweetcorn to a steamer, cover and cook over a saucepan of boiling water for 3 minutes. Plunge into cold water to cool quickly, then drain well and add to a bowl.

Add the red pepper, beansprouts, cooked rice noodles and shredded chicken to the bowl of steamed vegetables and mix together well.

To make the broth, add the stock, ground spices, star anise and soya sauce to a saucepan. Bring slowly to the boil, then simmer gently for 5 minutes. Taste and adjust the seasoning with salt and pepper if needed.

Divide the noodle mix between four serving bowls, ladle over the hot broth, sprinkle with the chopped coriander leaves and serve.

COOK'S TIP This recipe is gluten-free and dairy-free but read the back of the pack if using stock cubes, powdered bouillon or soy sauce as not all makes are gluten-free.

Brilliant baked beans

Serve these homemade baked beans on rustic sliced and toasted bread, spooned over a jacket potato with a sprinkling of grated cheese, or with a little grilled bacon for a late breakfast. Great for all ages.

Serves 4
Prep 10 minutes
Cook 30 minutes

1 tbsp vegetable oil

85g/3oz onions, finely
  chopped

85g/3oz carrots, cut into
  small dice

2 garlic cloves, finely chopped

2 tsp caster sugar

2 tsp red wine vinegar

4 tsp tomato purée

400g/14oz tomatoes, roughly
  chopped

Salt and pepper

2 x 400g/14oz can cannellini
  beans, drained, rinsed and
  drained again

Heat the oil in a saucepan, add the onion, carrots and garlic and fry over a medium heat for 10 minutes, stirring from time to time until the onions have softened and are just beginning to colour.

Increase the heat, stir in the sugar and continue to stir until the sugar has dissolved, then mix in the vinegar.

Reduce the heat to medium and stir in the tomato purée, chopped tomatoes and a little salt and pepper. Cook for 20 minutes, stirring from time to time until the tomatoes are very soft.

Remove the pan from the heat and blend with a stick blender or transfer to a liquidiser and blend until smooth, adding a little water, if needed, then return to the pan.

Stir in the cannellini beans and return to the heat. Cook until piping hot. Taste and adjust the seasoning and serve in bowls with warm bread and butter, on toast or spooned over a jacket potato.

COOK'S TIP If you are a fan of smoked paprika, stir 1 tsp of mild sweet paprika into the onions along with the tomato purée for kids, or for adults add hot smoked paprika, which has the same kind of kick as chilli powder. Top with chunky homemade guacamole and some fresh chopped coriander.

Goat's cheese & beetroot oatcake

These yeast-based griddle cakes are a little like large blinis and are made with finely ground porridge oats and flour. Top with a dill, horseradish and beetroot mix, wilted spinach and creamy goat's cheese mixed with yogurt for a light lunch.

Serves 4
Prep 30 minutes
Rise 1–1½ hours
Cook 11–20 minutes

OATCAKES
125g/4½oz porridge oats
125g/4½oz strong plain flour
1 tsp salt
1 tsp easy blend dried yeast
150ml/¼pt milk, lightly
    warmed
150ml/¼pt water, warmed
4–5 tsp vegetable oil

FOR THE BEETROOT
250g/9oz cooked, peeled
    beetroot, roughly chopped
2 tbsp natural yogurt
5g/2 sprigs fresh dill, finely
    chopped, plus a little extra
    for garnish, optional
10g/¼oz fresh horseradish,
    peeled, grated

TO FINISH
60g/2¼oz goat's cheese
85g/3oz natural yogurt
Little salt and pepper
100g/3½oz spinach
2 tsp sesame seeds, toasted
4 tsp pumpkin seeds

To make the oatcakes, blend the oats in a food processor or liquidiser until fine, then tip into a bowl. Add the flour, salt and yeast, stir well, then add the milk and whisk together. Gradually whisk in the water to make a smooth batter. Cover the top of the bowl with a tea towel or clingfilm and set aside in a warm place for 1–1½ hours.

Add the goat's cheese and yogurt to a food processor with a little salt and pepper and blend until smooth. Scoop into a bowl, cover with clingfilm and chill until needed.

Add the beetroot to the food processor, then add the yogurt, dill, horseradish and a little salt and pepper and pulse a few times to make a chunky purée. Spoon into a bowl, cover and set aside.

Rinse the spinach, shake off the water, then add to a frying pan and cook over a low heat for 3–4 minutes until just wilted and bright green. Set aside.

When the oatcake mixture is bubbly and risen brush the base of a large non-stick frying pan with a little oil. Add one quarter of the batter and spread into a circle about 12–15cm/5–6 inches in diameter. Cook for 1–2 minutes until the surface has large bubbles and the underside is golden, then flip over and cook the other side until golden.

Slide out of the pan and keep hot on a plate. Repeat to make four large oatcakes. Divide between four serving plates, top with the beetroot mix, the spinach and then top with spoonfuls of the goat's cheese yogurt. Garnish with sesame and pumpkin seeds and a few extra dill fronds, if liked. Serve with salad, or wild garlic if in season.

Pea & feta salad

This pretty salad makes the perfect light lunch and is even nicer if you can enjoy it in a sunny spot in the garden. If you have peas growing in the garden you can be extra generous with the pea shoots.

Serves 4
Prep 20 minutes
Cook 3 minutes

125g/4½oz podded fresh or
    frozen peas
125g/4½oz frozen edamame
    beans
85g/3oz mangetout
100g/3½oz carrots, thinly
    sliced
85g/3oz radishes, thinly sliced
10g/¼oz fresh mint, roughly
    torn
50g/1¾oz pea shoots
100g/3½oz feta cheese,
    drained, crumbled
60g/2¼oz cashew nuts,
    toasted, chopped

DRESSING
5 tbsp cold-pressed rapeseed
    oil
2 tbsp fresh chopped mint
4 tsp white wine vinegar
1 tsp caster sugar
Salt and pepper

Add the peas and edamame beans to a steamer then scatter the mangetout on top. Cover with a lid and steam above a saucepan of boiling water for 3 minutes. Plunge the vegetables into cold water to cool quickly, then drain well.

To make the dressing, spoon the oil into a small saucepan, add the chopped mint, white wine vinegar, sugar and a little salt and pepper. Bring just to a simmer over a medium heat, then leave to cool.

Add the carrots, radishes and torn mint leaves to a salad bowl. Pat the mangetout, peas and edamame beans dry with kitchen towel, then toss with the carrot mix. Roughly chop the pea shoots and gently toss with the other salad ingredients. Sprinkle with the feta cheese and cashew nuts. Fork the dressing together, then drizzle over the salad and serve.

COOK'S TIP Make sure to refresh the green vegetables after cooking by plunging into cold water, so that they keep bright green, then drain well.

If you don't have a steamer, add the vegetables to a saucepan of boiling salted water and cook for 1 minute then drain well.

Curried squash tarts

If you dislike making pastry, or feel you don't have the time, then these easy cheat tarts are for you. Simply unroll a sheet of puff pastry, cut into 6, then press into individual pudding tins… job done!

Makes 6
Prep 30 minutes
Cook 30–40 minutes
Cool 10 minutes

320g chilled ready rolled puff pastry sheet
Little flour, for dusting
250g/9oz butternut squash, deseeded, peeled, cut into small dice
2 tsp vegetable oil
125g/4½oz red onion, thinly sliced
1 garlic clove, finely chopped
10g/¼oz fresh coriander, chop stalks and leaves but keep separate
25g/1oz baby spinach leaves
1 tsp medium curry powder
Salt and pepper
150g/5oz natural yogurt
2 eggs
3 tbsp milk

Preheat the oven to 190°C/375°F/gas mark 5. Unroll the puff pastry and cut into six equal-sized pieces. With fingertips dusted in flour, lift one of the pastry squares into a 200ml/7fl oz individual metal pudding mould and press over the base and up the sides (don't worry if the top edges are a little uneven as they give a rustic look). Trim off the excess pastry and make 5 more tarts. Chill in the fridge while making the filling.

Steam the butternut squash above a saucepan of boiling water for 10 minutes until just softening. Alternatively, boil in a pan of water for 5 minutes and drain well.

Pour the oil into a frying pan, add the onion and fry over a medium heat for 5 minutes, stirring from time to time until softened. Add the garlic and chopped coriander stalks and fry for 2 minutes.

Add the butternut squash, spinach and curry powder to the onions and fry for 3 minutes until the spinach has just wilted, then season with salt and pepper.

Add the yogurt, eggs and milk to a bowl with the chopped coriander leaves and whisk together until smooth.

Pour half the yogurt mixture into the base of the pastry tarts. Divide the squash mixture between the pastry cases, then pour over the remaining yogurt mixture. Bake for 25–30 minutes until the filling is set and the pastry is golden. Leave to cool for 10 minutes, then loosen the tarts with a knife and remove from the tins. Serve warm or cold.

COOK'S TIP The puff pastry will rise during baking, unlike shortcrust, so don't be tempted to overfill the pies with the custard.

Minted pea & barley risotto

We usually think of pearl barley in meaty casseroles but it can also be used rather like rice in risottos, though pearl barley has much more fibre than white risotto rice.

Serves 4
Prep 20 minutes
Cook 42–44 minutes

15g/½oz butter
1 tbsp vegetable oil
150g/5½oz onions, finely chopped
2 garlic cloves, finely chopped
250g/9oz pearl barley
150ml/¼pt white wine
1 litre/1¾pt hot vegetable stock
350g/12oz frozen peas
100g/3½oz leek, thinly sliced
2 spring onions, thinly sliced
150g/5½oz frozen broad beans
3 tbsp fresh chopped parsley
3 tbsp fresh chopped mint
50g/1¾oz rocket leaves
100ml/3½fl oz double cream
Little freshly grated parmesan, to serve, optional

Heat the butter and oil in a large saucepan, add the onion and garlic and fry over a medium heat for 5 minutes, stirring until softened.

Mix in the pearl barley, stir to coat in the buttery juices and cook for 2 minutes. Pour in the wine and half the stock, bring to the boil, then reduce heat and simmer for 30 minutes, stirring from time to time and topping up with extra stock as needed, until the barley is tender and has absorbed most of the stock already added.

Defrost 150g/5oz of the peas in boiling water for a few minutes then drain, or use the microwave. Blend in a food processor or liquidiser to a coarse purée. Set aside.

Add the remaining peas, leeks, spring onions and broad beans to the risotto, top up with a little extra stock if needed, then cook for 3–4 minutes until the vegetables are hot and tender. Stir in the puréed peas, chopped herbs, most of the rocket leaves and cream. Adjust with a little extra stock if needed and cook for 2–3 minutes until the rocket has just wilted and the risotto has a creamy texture. Taste and adjust the seasoning with extra salt and pepper if needed. Spoon into bowls and top with the remaining rocket and grated parmesan, if liked.

COOK'S TIP Grow your own mint and parsley in pots on the windowsill or doorstep for an ever-ready supply of herbs. Even if you have a garden, mint is still best grown in a pot or a pot sunk into the flowerbed so that it doesn't become too invasive.

For a pop of bright green colour, you can pod the broad beans before adding them to the risotto.

Broccoli & feta parcels

Wafer-thin filo pastry is so easy to use — simply unwrap, unfold and layer in a baking tin, brushing the layers with a little melted butter. Fill with a feta, cottage cheese and fresh chopped dill mix speckled with broccoli. Delicious served warm from the oven with a crisp salad for a light lunch.

Serves 4–6
Prep 30 minutes
Cook 30–35 minutes

170g/6oz broccoli, cut into
   small florets, stalks diced
70g/2½oz onion, finely
   chopped
100g/3½oz feta cheese,
   drained, crumbled into
   small pieces
55g/2oz cottage cheese
2 tbsp fresh chopped dill
2 eggs, beaten
½ tsp grated nutmeg
Salt and pepper
270g/9½oz pack chilled
   filo pastry
70g/2½oz butter, melted

Preheat the oven to 180°C/350°F/gas mark 4. Add the broccoli and onion to a large bowl, then add the feta cheese, cottage cheese and dill. Pour in the eggs, season with nutmeg and some salt and pepper and mix together.

Unfold the filo pastry, lay two sheets into a 18 x 28 x 4cm/7 x 11 x 1½ inch small roasting tin or fixed-base shallow cake tin and brush with butter. Continue layering and buttering until you have two sheets of filo left.

Spoon the broccoli mix over the pastry. Fold any pastry that is hanging over the sides of the tin over the filling, brushing with butter, then lay the remaining pastry over the top, folding and pleating the pastry to give a rumpled effect. Brush with the remaining butter.

Bake for 30–35 minutes until golden brown. Leave to cool then cut into squares and serve warm or cold with salad.

COOK'S TIP Filo pastry dries very quickly once taken out of its wrapper, so separate the sheets and layer up immediately. If you have to leave midway through, then cover the unused sheets with dampened kitchen roll or a dampened tea towel. Any remaining pastry in the pack can be re-wrapped in clingfilm and frozen for another time.

Garlic fans can try adding 1–2 finely chopped garlic cloves to the broccoli mix.

Carrot, cauliflower, kale & pomegranate tabbouleh

This robust hearty salad stores well in the fridge and is a good way to use up the tail end of the winter vegetables in the kitchen garden or allotment. Sissinghurst in Kent and Ickworth in Suffolk both have bountiful kitchen gardens, just waiting to be explored.

Serves 4–6
Prep 20 minutes
Cook 20 minutes

170g/6oz pearl barley
¾ tsp ground cinnamon
100ml/3 ½ fl oz cold-pressed
  rapeseed oil
4 tsp white wine vinegar
Salt and pepper
125g/4oz carrot, coarsely
  grated
½ small cauliflower, cut into
  small florets, washed well
1 orange, juice only
125g/4 ½ oz kale, very thinly
  sliced
1 pomegranate, seeds only
70g/2 ½ oz walnut pieces,
  chopped
30g/1oz flat-leaf parsley,
  roughly chopped
15g/½ oz mint, roughly
  chopped

Rinse the pearl barley with cold water, add to a saucepan with the cinnamon, cover with water and bring to the boil. Cook for 20 minutes or until the barley is tender.

Add the oil and vinegar to a large bowl with a little salt and pepper and whisk together. Drain the pearl barley and add while still hot to the dressing, toss together then put to one side to cool.

Add the carrot and cauliflower to a second bowl, pour over the orange juice and mix together. Add the pearl barley, kale, pomegranate seeds, walnuts and herbs and toss together until well mixed, then serve.

COOK'S TIP As the cauliflower is served raw it is essential to ensure it is properly cleaned in plenty of cold water before use, then drain well and shake off any water.

Watercress scones with smoked trout pâté

We try to include as many local ingredients as we can in our café menus. These delicious savoury scones were developed by the chefs at Hinton Ampner, using ingredients from the walled garden and locally sourced Hampshire trout and watercress.

Makes 8
Prep 30 minutes
Cook 12–15 minutes

FOR THE SCONES
340g/12oz self-raising flour
100g/3½oz butter or
    margarine, diced, plus extra
    for greasing
40g/1½oz watercress,
    chopped
Salt and pepper
1 egg, beaten
120ml/4fl oz milk

FOR THE PÂTÉ
250g/9oz hot smoked trout
140g/5oz full fat soft cheese
70g/2½oz red onion, thinly
    sliced
115g/4oz fennel, thinly sliced
2 tsp fresh chopped dill

TO SERVE
40g/1½oz cucumber, finely
    diced
40g/1½oz tomato, finely
    diced
2 tbsp fresh chopped
    watercress
80g/2¼oz mixed leaf salad,
    or watercress

First make the scones. Preheat the oven to 200°C/400°F/gas mark 6. Add the flour and butter or margarine to a bowl and rub in with fingertips or an electric mixer until the mixture resembles fine crumbs.

Stir in the watercress and a little salt and pepper. Mix together the egg and milk, then (saving a tablespoon back for the glaze) gradually mix in just enough of this mixture to make a soft but not sticky dough. Lightly knead on a floured surface, then roll out to a 2cm/¾ inch thickness. Stamp out with a 7cm/2¼ inch biscuit cutter. Place onto a greased baking sheet, leaving a little space between the scones for them to rise. Re-roll trimmings and continue until you have 8 scones.

Brush the scone tops with the remaining egg, then bake for 10–15 minutes until well risen and golden.

While the scones cook, make the pâté. Flake the trout into pieces with a knife and fork and discard any bones. Add to a mixing bowl with the soft cheese, red onion, fennel and dill and mix together to a rough-textured pâté. Season to taste with a little salt and pepper. Spoon into a bowl or clip top jar. Cover and chill until ready to serve.

Mix the diced cucumber, tomato and remaining watercress to make a salsa-style accompaniment.

Serve the scones while still warm with spoonfuls of the pâté, the salsa and a little salad.

Sausage bubble & squeak

Sausage and mash is proper comfort food. Rather than just mashed potato and cabbage in the bubble & squeak, carrots, parsnips, fried onions and bacon have also been added for an extra kick of flavour.

Serves 4
Prep 25 minutes
Cook 50–60 minutes

450g/1lb potatoes, washed and chopped
400g/14oz carrots, peeled and roughly cut
170g/6oz parsnips, peeled and roughly cut
2 tbsp vegetable oil
115g/4oz onion, chopped
70g/2½oz smoked back bacon, diced
170g/6oz green cabbage, shredded
Salt and pepper
10g/¼oz butter or dairy-free margarine, melted
800g/1¾lb or 12 pork sausages

FOR THE GRAVY
1 tbsp vegetable oil
300g/10½oz red onions, thinly sliced
1 tbsp caster sugar
4 tbsp red wine
250ml/9fl oz beef stock
1 tbsp cornflour

Preheat the oven to 190°C/375°F/gas mark 5. Add the potatoes, carrots and parsnips to a saucepan of boiling water and simmer for 15–20 minutes until soft then drain well and return to the pan.

Meanwhile, heat 1 tablespoon of oil in a frying pan, add the onion and fry over a medium heat for 10 minutes, stirring from time to time until softened and just beginning to colour. Add the bacon, increase the heat slightly and fry the bacon for 4–5 minutes until cooked.

Add the cabbage to a saucepan of boiling water, cook for 3–4 minutes until just tender and still bright green. Drain and cool quickly under cold water then drain again.

Roughly mash the root vegetables in the pan until broken down. Stir in the onion, bacon and cabbage and season with salt and pepper. Press into an oiled ovenproof dish and brush the top with the melted butter or margarine.

Brush a roasting tin with 1 tablespoon oil then add the sausages in a single layer. Put the sausages into the oven on a higher shelf with the vegetable dish on the shelf below. Bake for 35–40 minutes, turning several times until the sausages are evenly browned and the vegetables are hot and slightly crispy on top.

For the gravy, heat the oil in the frying pan, add the onions and fry over a medium heat for 5 minutes until just softened. Stir in the sugar and cook for 5–10 minutes until the sugar has dissolved and caramelised. Stir in the red wine, cook for 1 minute then mix in the stock. Bring to the boil, then simmer for 5 minutes. Mix the cornflour to a smooth paste with a little water and stir into the gravy. Cook until thickened, then add salt and pepper.

Spoon the bubble and squeak cake onto plates, top each portion with three sausages, then spoon the gravy around and serve.

Beef, prune & orange tagine

Marinate the beef with tomatoes, onions, garlic and a mellow mix of spices the day before to really add flavour, then slowly cook with orange juice, stock and honey for beef that is meltingly tender.

Serves 4
Prep 20 minutes
Marinate 2 hours or overnight
Cook 2 hours 50 minutes–3
hours

500g/1lb 2oz lean stewing
    beef, diced
¼ tsp salt
250g/9oz tomatoes, chopped
200g/7oz onions, finely
    chopped
2–3 garlic cloves, finely
    chopped
2 tbsp rapeseed oil
1 tsp ground cumin
1 tsp ground coriander
1½ tsp ground ginger
½ tsp dried chilli flakes
100ml/3½fl oz orange juice
30g/1oz fresh coriander, chop
    the stalks and leaves but
    keep separate
600ml/1pt beef stock
100g/3½oz pitted prunes
2 tsp honey

In a large bowl mix together the meat, salt, tomatoes, onions, garlic, oil and all the spices. Cover and chill for 2 hours or longer if possible.

Add the marinated meat to a large saucepan and cook uncovered over a medium heat for 20–30 minutes, stirring occasionally. Add the orange juice, coriander stalks and enough stock to cover.

Cover and simmer gently for 2 hours, stirring occasionally until the beef is tender. Stir in the prunes, honey and coriander leaves and cook for a further 30 minutes.

Spoon into bowls and serve with cous cous or mashed potato.

COOK'S TIP Keep an eye on the tagine as it cooks and stir a little more frequently towards the end of cooking as the sauce thickens. If the sauce seems very thick when you add the prunes, top up with a little more stock or water.

If you would rather, the tagine can be cooked in the oven at 160°C/325°F/gas mark 3 for the same time, just reduce the amount of stock down to 450ml/¾pt.

Vegetable & coconut curry

Comfort food needn't just mean meaty casseroles – this mellow, full-flavoured curry is packed with a mix of root vegetables, cauliflower and spinach with zingy fresh herbs and chickpeas. Serve with naan, flatbreads or rice.

Serves 4
Prep 20 minutes
Cook 30–45 minutes

1 tbsp vegetable oil
200g/7oz onions, chopped
1 garlic clove, finely chopped
15g/½oz fresh coriander, chop
  stalks and leaves but keep
  separate
55g/2oz tikka masala paste
100g/3½oz carrots, cut into
  1cm/½inch dice
250g/9oz potatoes, cut into
  1cm/½inch dice
¼ cauliflower or 115g/4oz
  florets, cut into small pieces
450ml/16fl oz vegetable stock
  or water
2 tsp caster sugar
½ tsp ground cinnamon
2 cardamom pods, crushed
55g/2oz spinach
½ x 400g/14oz can full fat
  coconut milk
400g/14oz can chickpeas,
  drained, rinsed with cold
  water and drained again
2 tsp fresh chopped mint
Salt
1 tbsp mango chutney, plus
  extra to serve

Heat the oil in a saucepan, add the onion, garlic, coriander stalks and tikka masala paste and cook over a medium heat for 5–10 minutes, stirring from time to time until the onions are softened.

Stir in the carrots, potatoes and cauliflower, then add the stock or water, half the sugar, the cinnamon and cardamom pods and seeds, so that the liquid just covers the vegetables. Bring to the boil, then cover and simmer for 20–30 minutes until the vegetables are just soft.

Add the spinach leaves, coconut milk, chickpeas and mint. Stir well, season with a little salt, then stir in the rest of the sugar and 1 tablespoon mango chutney. Bring back to the boil and cook for 5 minutes. Ladle into bowls, sprinkle with the remaining coriander leaves and extra teaspoonfuls of mango chutney. Serve with warm naan or rice.

COOK'S TIP You might like to try this curry with homemade fennel flatbreads that accompany the Butter Chicken (see page 122).

Cappuccino cake

Coffee cake is always popular. In a busy week we can sell up to 700 slices of cake at Fountains Abbey, North Yorkshire, our largest café. This version is both gluten-free and dairy-free.

Cuts into 8 slices
Prep 30 minutes
Cook 25 minutes

225g/9oz dairy-free margarine
200g/7oz caster sugar
4 eggs
225g/8oz gluten-free
   self-raising flour
1 tsp gluten-free baking
   powder
4 tsp instant coffee dissolved
   in 4 tsp boiling water

FROSTING
140g/5oz dairy-free soft
   margarine
250g/9oz icing sugar
4 tsp instant coffee dissolved
   in 4 tsp boiling water
1 tbsp soya milk or water,
   optional
1 tsp cocoa

Preheat the oven to 180°C/350°F/gas mark 4. Grease two 20cm/ 8 inch sandwich tins and line the bases with a circle of non-stick baking paper.

Cream the margarine and sugar together in the bowl of your mixer until light and fluffy. Add the eggs, one at a time, beating well between each addition and spooning in a little flour to stop the mixture from separating.

Gradually mix in the remaining flour and baking powder, then add the dissolved coffee and beat until smooth.

Divide the mixture between the two cake tins, level the surface and bake for 25 minutes until well risen and the tops spring back when gently pressed with a fingertip. Leave to cool in the tins for 5 minutes then loosen the edges and turn out on to a cooling rack.

To make the frosting, add the margarine to the bowl of your mixer then gradually mix in the icing sugar until smooth and fluffy. Mix in the dissolved coffee and the soya milk or water, if needed, to make a soft spreadable icing.

Peel away the lining paper from the cakes, then sandwich the cakes together with a little of the frosting. Put the cake onto a serving plate then spread a thin layer of frosting over the top and sides of the cake to stick the crumbs in place. Spread a thicker layer of frosting over the sides then swirl the remainder over the top. Dust with sifted cocoa and cut into slices to serve.

Banana & cardamom bake

We have all been caught out at some time and forgotten to eat the bananas when we should have done. This easy recipe is a great way to use up those brown speckled bananas in the fruit bowl – they may not look their best but they will taste wonderfully sweet.

Cuts into 10 bars
Prep 30 minutes
Cook 30–35 minutes

300g/10½oz self-raising flour
6 cardamom pods, crushed,
    pods discarded, black seeds
    ground in a pestle and
    mortar
1 tsp ground mixed spice
1 tsp bicarbonate of soda
Pinch salt
680g/1½lb or 4 medium
    bananas, weighed with
    skins on
115g/4oz butter or soft
    margarine
85g/3oz caster sugar
3 eggs
2 tbsp milk
1 tsp vanilla extract
70g/2½oz sultanas

TO DECORATE
55g/2oz caster sugar
2 tbsp water
15g/½oz butter
55g/2oz icing sugar
1½–2 tsp water

Preheat the oven to 180°C/350°F/gas mark 4. Line the base and sides of a 18 x 28 x 4cm/7 x 11 x 1½ inch shallow cake tin with a large piece of non-stick baking paper, snip diagonally into the corners then press the paper into the tin so that the base and sides are lined.

Add the flour, crushed cardamom seeds, mixed spice, bicarbonate of soda and salt to a bowl and mix together. Peel the bananas, chop half and mash the rest on a plate with a fork.

Cream the margarine and sugar together in the bowl of your mixer until light and fluffy. Add the eggs, one at a time, with a spoonful of the flour mix, beating well after each addition. Then gradually beat in the remaining flour, milk and vanilla.

Add the bananas and sultanas and gently mix together. Spoon into the lined tin and bake for 25–30 minutes until well risen and golden brown and a skewer inserted into the centre comes out cleanly. Leave to cool in the tin for 5 minutes then transfer to a wire rack to cool completely.

Remove the lining paper from the cake and transfer to a board. Add the caster sugar and water to a small saucepan, heat gently without stirring until the sugar has dissolved, tilting the pan to mix rather than using a spoon. Increase the heat and cook, still without stirring for about 5 minutes until the syrup has turned to a thick golden caramel. Take off the heat, add the butter and stir together with a wooden spoon, then drizzle over the top of the cake in squiggly lines. Leave to cool and set for 15 minutes or so.

Sift the icing sugar into a bowl, stir in just enough water to make a smooth spoonable icing, then drizzle over the cake. Leave to set, then cut into bars to serve.

Rhubarb shortbread & ginger cream

The early pink rhubarb stems loved by the Victorians were originally forced on in candlelit sheds or under tall pottery domes in the kitchen garden. Their delicate colour really lifts the spirits after the long days of winter.

Makes 6
Prep 30 minutes
Cook 26–34 minutes

100g/3½oz plain flour
50g/1¾oz cornflour
50g/1¾oz caster sugar
100g/3½oz butter

RHUBARB COMPOTE

70ml/2½ fl oz red wine
70ml/2½ fl oz water
70g/2½oz caster sugar
¾ tsp ground ginger
340g/12oz forced rhubarb,
    trimmed, cut into
    4cm/1½inch lengths

TOPPING

300ml/10fl oz double cream
150g/5½oz natural yogurt

Preheat the oven to 160°C/325°F/gas mark 3. Add the flour, cornflour, sugar and butter to a bowl and rub in with fingertips or a mixer until fine crumbs. Continue to mix and squeeze the crumbs together to make a ball, then lightly knead.

Roll out thinly. Try placing two boards either side of the rolling pin to ensure an even thickness. Trim to a rectangle 30 x 10cm/12 x 4 inch. Cut into six rectangles, each 7.5 x 5cm/3 x 2 inch. Transfer to a baking sheet, prick the biscuits with a fork and bake for 20–25 minutes until straw coloured and firm. Neaten the edges with a serrated knife if needed, then leave to cool.

To make the compote, add the red wine, water, sugar and ginger to a small frying pan and bring to the boil, stirring until the sugar has dissolved. Add the rhubarb, cook for 1 minute, then turn off the heat and leave to cool and continue cooking in the liquid until just softened but holding their shape.

Place a sieve over a bowl, tip the rhubarb mix into the sieve then pour the juices from the bowl back into the frying pan and reduce until thickened and syrupy and you have about 6 tablespoons.

Whip the cream in a second bowl until it forms firm peaks, then fold in the yogurt. Transfer the shortbread biscuits to individual serving plates and stick to the plates with a small dot of cream. Pipe or spoon two layers of the cream over the biscuits. Arrange the rhubarb side by side on the top, then drizzle with a little of the wine syrup and serve.

Apple & rhubarb crumble

*Everyone, young and old, loves warm crumble and custard. Oats and a little
ground ginger have been added to the topping for a little twist on an old favourite.*

Serves 4
Prep 20 minutes
Cook 25–30 minutes

375g/13oz cooking apples,
  peeled, quartered, cored,
  diced
250g/9oz trimmed rhubarb,
  cut into 2cm/¾ inch slices
25g/1oz caster sugar
15g/½ oz plain flour

FOR THE TOPPING
125g/4½ oz plain flour
25g/1oz oats
25g/1oz caster sugar
80g/2¾ oz butter or soft
  margarine, diced
1½ tsp ground ginger
2 tbsp soft light brown sugar

Preheat the oven to 180°C/350°F/gas mark 4. Add the apples and
rhubarb to the base of a 1.2ltr/2pt ovenproof dish. Sprinkle over the
sugar and flour and mix together.

To make the topping, add the flour, oats, sugar and butter or
margarine to a bowl with the ginger. Rub the fat into the flour with
fingertips or an electric mixer until it resembles fine crumbs.

Spoon the crumble over the fruit in an even layer then sprinkle with
the brown sugar. Bake for 25–30 minutes until the top is golden.
Spoon into bowls and serve with hot custard.

COOK'S TIP The crumble topping freezes well in a plastic
bag or plastic container and can be used straight from the freezer,
no need to defrost first, just add an extra 5–10 minutes on to the
cooking time.

Gin & tonic cake

Our chef at Powis Castle café has taken a lime drizzle loaf to another level with the addition of G&T!
Quinine is essential to make tonic, and this was imported by Robert Clive of the East India Company.
He lived at the castle in Powys and built up one of the largest collections of Indian treasures in the UK.

Cuts into 10 slices
Prep 30 minutes
Cook 55–60 minutes

200g/7oz unsalted butter,
   softened, plus extra to
   grease
200g/7oz caster sugar
4 eggs, beaten
200g/7oz self-raising flour
½ tsp baking powder
1 lime, finely grated zest only
85ml/3fl oz gin

DRIZZLE AND ICING
125g/4½oz caster sugar
120ml/4fl oz tonic water
3½ tbsp gin
1 lime, cut in half lengthways
   and very thinly sliced into
   half moons
100g/3½oz icing sugar, sifted

Preheat oven to 180°C/350°F/gas mark 4. Grease a 900g/2lb loaf tin with a little butter then line the base and two long sides with a piece of non-stick baking paper.

Cream the butter and sugar together in a large bowl with an electric mixer until light and fluffy. Gradually add the eggs, beating well after each addition and spooning in a little of the flour to stop the mixture from separating.

Fold in the remaining flour, baking powder and lime zest, then gradually add the gin. Spoon into the prepared tin, level the surface and bake for 55–60 minutes or until a skewer inserted into the centre comes out clean.

Meanwhile, make the sugar syrup: gently heat the caster sugar and tonic water in a small pan, stirring often, until the sugar dissolves. Turn up the heat and boil for 1 minute. Spoon 2 tablespoons of the syrup into a small bowl and mix in 2 tablespoons of the gin (this mixture will be used to soak the loaf later).

Add the thinly sliced lime to the remaining tonic syrup in the saucepan. Bring to the boil and cook for 5–7 minutes until the lime slices are soft and the syrup thickened. Spoon the lime slices over a baking sheet lined with non-stick baking paper, draining off some of the syrup and leave to cool.

As soon as the loaf comes out of the oven, poke holes into the top with a skewer and drizzle over the reserved gin syrup from the bowl. Cool the loaf in the tin on a wire rack.

Make the icing by mixing together the sifted icing sugar with the remaining 1½ tablespoons gin until smooth. Remove the loaf from tin, transfer to a board and peel off the paper. Spoon over the icing and decorate with the lime slices. Leave the cake to set before slicing.

Salted caramel mousse

This dessert is a little like chocolate millionaire's shortbread in a glass – incredibly rich and delicious. Best of all, it is gluten-free so no one need miss out.

Serves 6
Prep 40 minutes
Cook 10–15 minutes
Chill 4 hours

BISCUIT BASE
140g/5oz gluten-free plain
   flour
70g 2½oz butter, diced, or
   soft margarine
30g/1oz caster sugar

MOUSSE
20g/¾oz cornflour
30g/1oz cocoa
40g/1½oz caster sugar
200ml/7fl oz milk
20g/¾oz butter
150ml/¼pt double cream
Pinch salt

CARAMEL
100g/3½oz caster sugar
2 tbsp water
85ml/3fl oz double cream
Pinch salt

TOPPING
15g/½oz dark chocolate,
   chopped
Pinch coarse salt

Preheat the oven to 180°C/350°F/gas mark 4. To make the base, add the flour, butter or margarine and sugar to a bowl and rub in with fingertips until it resembles fine crumbs. Squeeze together roughly to make a loose dough with rough clumps. Tip onto a baking sheet and spread into an even layer. Bake for 10–15 minutes until crisp and golden. Check halfway through cooking and stir the outer edges to the centre as these will cook more quickly. Leave to cool.

To make the mousse, add the cornflour, cocoa and sugar to a bowl then mix to a smooth paste with a little of the milk. Pour the rest of the milk into a saucepan, stir in the cornflour mixture and cook over a low heat, slowly bringing to the boil and stirring constantly until thickened, smooth and glossy. Stir in the butter until melted then spoon into a clean bowl, cover with clingfilm and leave to cool.

For the caramel, add the sugar to a heavy based saucepan with the water, cook over a medium heat until the sugar dissolves, tilting and swirling the pan, rather than stirring, until it forms a clear syrup. Continue to cook for about 3 minutes without stirring, until the syrup changes to an even golden brown.

Take the pan off the heat and gradually pour in the cream in a thin steady stream. It will bubble vigorously, so stand well back. Stir to make a smooth caramel sauce, sprinkle in the salt and leave to cool.

Whip the cream for the mousse in a bowl until it forms soft swirls. Add one third to the cooled cocoa mixture with a pinch of salt and gently stir together to loosen the mix. Gently whisk in the remaining cream until the mousse is thick and creamy.

Crush the cooled biscuit base and divide between six small wine glasses or glass dishes. Spoon or pipe the mousse into the dishes. Spoon or pipe the caramel over the top of the mousse, swirling the glass to ensure an even layer covers the top of the dish. Sprinkle each dish with a little chopped chocolate and a tiny pinch of salt.

St Clement's sponge

Steamed puddings just epitomise comfort food. These individual lemony sponge puddings are topped with lemon and orange curd and a drizzle of hot custard. The puddings freeze and reheat well in the microwave, then top with the St Clement's curd just before serving.

Serves 4
Prep 2 minutes
Cook 40 minutes

100g/3½oz butter or soft
  margarine
100g/3½oz caster sugar
2 eggs
100g/3½oz self-raising flour
½ lemon, grated zest and
  juice
140g/5oz St Clement's curd

Brush the inside of four 200ml/7fl oz individual metal pudding moulds with a little oil and line the bases with a circle of non-stick baking paper.

Add the butter, sugar, eggs, flour, lemon zest and juice to the bowl of your mixer and whisk until light and fluffy and pale in colour.

Divide the mixture evenly between the tins, spread the tops level, then tap each mould on the work surface.

Loosely cover the tops with clingfilm or squares of oiled foil, doming up the foil to allow for the puddings to rise a little. Put the puddings in a steamer, cover with a lid and set over a saucepan of simmering water. Steam for about 40 minutes until well risen or until a skewer inserted into the centre comes out cleanly.

Warm the St Clement's curd in a small saucepan over a low heat or in the microwave until a soft dropping consistency. Turn the puddings out into shallow bowls, spoon over the warm St Clement's curd and serve with custard.

COOK'S TIP St Clement's curd is a mix of lemon and orange zest and juices and is sold in our National Trust shops. If you can't find it locally then buy lemon curd and stir in a little finely grated orange zest when warming at the end of the recipe.

Jam roly-poly

Roly-poly always puts a smile on the faces of our visitors – bringing back memories of granny, a favourite auntie or school lunches. Forget about steaming for hours with windows running with condensation, this easy version is baked in a large loaf tin in the oven.

Serves 8
Prep 20 minutes
Cook 40–55 minutes

Butter, for greasing
300g/10½oz self-raising flour
150g/5½oz vegetable suet
40g/1½oz caster sugar
200–250ml/7–9fl oz water
225g/8oz raspberry jam

Preheat the oven to 180°C/350°F/gas mark 4. Butter a 900g/2lb loaf tin and line the base and two long sides with one piece of non-stick baking paper.

Mix the flour, suet and sugar together in a bowl, then gradually stir in enough water to make a soft but not sticky dough that leaves the sides of the bowl clean.

Lightly knead the dough on a lightly floured surface then roll out and trim to a rectangle 40 x 23cm/16 x 9 inch (or, if you put the loaf tin in the centre of the pastry, the short side is the length of the loaf tin and the long side is three times the base width of the tin).

Spread the jam over the pastry leaving a 2cm/¾ inch border all round. Roll up the dough from one short side to the other, then lift the roll into the tin. Cover the top of the tin loosely with buttered foil so that it is slightly domed up and folded over the edges of the tin. Bake in the oven for 40–55 minutes or until well risen and a skewer comes out cleanly from the centre. Remove the foil for the last 5–10 minutes so that the top can brown a little, if liked.

Leave to stand for 5–10 minutes. Loosen the edge of the roly-poly and lift out of the tin using the lining paper. Cut into thick slices, transfer to serving plates and serve with hot custard.

COOK'S TIP If you have half an orange or half a lemon it can be nice to stir a little grated fruit zest into the suet pastry before adding the water.

Summer

Relax and unwind in the summer sun with a family picnic on the beach or woodland walk, and take along our extra special Picnic Pie with Relish and Raspberry & White Chocolate Muffins. For something a little more romantic, enjoy the heady perfumes and colours of English roses in one of our lovely gardens, then head home for an elegant supper of Open Ravioli with Egg & Spinach Cream Sauce, Seasonal Goat's Cheese Gnocchi or Tandoori Chicken with a tangy summer slaw. Dust off the best china and spoil yourself with a slice of Courgette, Lemon & Thyme sponge, or Raspberry Rippled Cheesecake Cake with a cup of tea served in the garden.

Broad bean minestrone soup

Light, fresh and full of flavour, soup needn't be just for winter. Mix and match the vegetables depending on what you have, or what you are growing in the garden or allotment, for this main meal. If you don't eat meat, just leave out the bacon and add two finely chopped garlic cloves instead, being sure to use a vegetarian pesto.

Serves 4
Prep 15 minutes
Cook 38 minutes

1 tbsp vegetable oil
55g/2oz smoked back bacon, diced
200g/7oz onions, chopped
2 sticks celery, chopped
200g/7oz carrots, chopped
1 bay leaf
1.2ltr/2pt chicken or vegetable stock
Salt and pepper
70g/2½oz dried spaghetti, roughly crushed
140g/5oz broad beans, fresh or frozen
140g/5oz green beans, sliced
55g/2oz green cabbage, chopped
4 tsp green pesto
Fresh basil leaves to garnish, optional

Heat the oil in a saucepan, add the bacon and fry over a medium heat for 5 minutes, stirring until just beginning to brown. Mix in the onions, celery and carrots and fry for a further 10 minutes, stirring from time to time.

Add the bay leaf and pour in the stock, season with a little salt and pepper and bring to the boil. Cover and simmer for about 15 minutes until the vegetables are soft.

Sprinkle in the crushed pasta and bring back to the boil. Cook for 5 minutes until the pasta is just soft. Add the broad beans, green beans and cabbage, then stir the pesto through the soup. Cook for 3 minutes. Remove the bay leaf, taste and adjust the seasoning if needed, and ladle into bowls. Garnish with basil leaves and add extra pesto to taste, if liked. Serve with crusty bread and butter.

COOK'S TIP If using fresh broad beans, you can remove the outer casing for a brighter green colour in the soup.

This soup is best served soon after making so that the green vegetables stay bright green. If it is left to stand you will find that the pasta will just keep on swelling and growing so you will need to adjust with a little extra stock.

Vegetable soup

Packed with different vegetables, this tasty soup is an easy way to boost your five a day.

Serves 4–6
Prep 20 minutes
Cook 25 minutes

1 tbsp vegetable oil
150g/5½oz onions, chopped
150g/5½oz carrots, chopped
150g/5½oz broccoli, chopped
125g/4½oz courgettes, chopped
150g/5½oz fresh podded or frozen peas
200g/7oz potatoes, chopped
700ml/1¼pt vegetable stock
1 tsp dried mixed herbs
Salt and pepper
Carrot shavings, to garnish

Heat the oil in a saucepan, add all the vegetables and fry over a medium heat for 5 minutes, stirring until softened but not coloured.

Pour in the stock, add the herbs and a little salt and pepper and bring to the boil. Cover and simmer for 15 minutes until the vegetables are tender but still brightly coloured.

Purée in the saucepan with a stick blender or transfer to a liquidiser and blend until smooth, then return to the pan. Reheat if necessary. Taste and adjust the seasoning, adding a little more stock if needed.

Ladle into bowls and garnish with carrot shavings.

COOK'S TIP To make carrot shavings, peel away wafer-thin slices of carrot with a swivel-bladed vegetable peeler, running down the length of the carrot.

Ham, bean & barley salad

Mustard is one of those underused condiments that we all have in the cupboard. Rather than just serving as something on the side, here it is the mainstay of this peppery dressing, adding a delicate pale yellow colour that belies its fiery kick. While barley and ham may not sound like a usual salad combination it makes a great main course salad.

Serves 4–6
Prep 20 minutes
Cook 20 minutes

140g/5oz pearl barley
140g/5oz green beans, cut
    into thirds
100g/3½oz fresh podded or
    frozen peas
85g/3oz radicchio, thinly
    sliced
25g/1oz flat-leaf parsley,
    roughly chopped
60g/2¼oz rocket leaves
225g/8oz ham, shredded

DRESSING
3 tsp English mustard
3 tsp wholegrain mustard
4 tsp white wine vinegar
40g/1½oz mayonnaise
4 tbsp apple juice
55g/2oz red onion, finely
    chopped
Salt and pepper

Add the pearl barley to a saucepan, cover with cold water and bring to the boil. Simmer for 20 minutes, stirring occasionally until the barley is tender, then drain into a sieve, rinse with cold water and leave to drain in the sieve.

Meanwhile, add the green beans and peas to a saucepan of boiling water and cook for 2 minutes. Drain well, then plunge into cold water, then drain again.

Add the drained barley, beans and peas to a salad bowl, then add the radicchio and parsley and gently toss together.

To make the dressing, add the English and wholegrain mustard to a smaller bowl with the vinegar and mayonnaise and whisk together. Gradually whisk in the apple juice until smooth, then mix in the chopped onion and salt and pepper to taste.

Add the rocket leaves and shredded ham to the salad, then pour over the dressing, gently toss together and serve.

COOK'S TIP Don't add the dressing, ham and rocket leaves to the salad until the last minute.

Not all supermarkets sell radicchio unless it is mixed into bags of ready prepared salad. If you cannot find it whole then substitute a small red- or green-tipped spear of chicory.

Tomato & fennel soup

Tomato soup is a favourite with most people. If you haven't tried it with a little fresh fennel then I can really recommend it, as it adds a delicate aniseed flavour that brings out the full flavour of the ripe, summer tomatoes.

Serves 4–6
Prep 20 minutes
Cook 25 minutes

1 tbsp vegetable oil
200g/7oz onions, chopped
1 medium sized fennel bulb,
   chop 150g/4½oz (thinly
   shred remainder and reserve
   along with any green fronds
   for garnish)
80g/2¾oz tomato paste
115g/4oz carrots, diced
400g/14oz fresh tomatoes,
   diced
500ml/18fl oz vegetable stock
Salt and pepper
1 tsp red wine vinegar
2 tbsp extra virgin rapeseed oil
   to garnish
½ tsp fennel seeds

Heat the oil in a saucepan, add the onion and chopped fennel and fry over a medium heat for 5 minutes, stirring from time to time until softened but not browned. Stir in the tomato purée and fry for 5 minutes, stirring.

Add the carrots and tomatoes, stir well and fry for 5 minutes until the tomatoes are beginning to break down.

Pour in the stock and a little salt and pepper and bring to the boil. Cover and simmer for about 10 minutes until the carrots are soft and the tomatoes pulpy.

Add the vinegar and purée the soup still in the pan with a stick blender, or transfer to a liquidiser and blend until smooth then return to the pan. Adjust the consistency with a little extra stock or water and extra seasoning if needed.

Place the oil in a small pan and heat gently, add the fennel seeds, remove from the heat and leave to cool slightly.

Reheat and ladle into bowls. Drizzle with a little oil and sprinkle over a little shredded fennel and green fennel fronds to serve.

All day breakfast omelette

Transform a couple of leftover cooked sausages and two smallish leftover potatoes into this tasty oven baked omelette. Just the thing for a late weekend breakfast, to pack into a container to eat while out and about, or to sustain hungry kids after football practice.

Serves 4
Prep 20 minutes
Cook 32–47 minutes

1 tbsp vegetable oil
150g/5 ½ oz mushrooms,
  quartered
115g/4oz smoked back bacon,
  diced
2 cooked pork sausages, sliced
6 eggs
3 tbsp milk
2 tbsp fresh chopped parsley
115g/4oz cooked potatoes,
  diced
Salt and pepper

Preheat the oven to 180°C/350°F/gas mark 4. Use a large piece of non-stick baking paper to line the base and sides of a 20cm/8 inch shallow, square, fixed-base cake tin, folding the paper into the corners so that it fits snugly.

Heat the oil in the frying pan, add the mushrooms and bacon and fry for 5–10 minutes over a medium heat, increasing the heat as the mushrooms begin to release their liquid. Continue to cook until the mushrooms are dry and the bacon cooked. Add the sausages and cook for 2 minutes.

Beat the eggs, milk, parsley and some salt and pepper together in a bowl. Add the mushrooms, bacon and potatoes and stir together.

Pour into the lined tin and bake for about 25–35 minutes until the omelette is set and golden brown on top. Leave to stand for 5 minutes.

Lift the omelette out of the tin holding the paper, put onto a chopping board, cut into squares and lift off the paper. Serve warm or cold.

COOK'S TIP Not a fan of mushrooms? Add the same weight of diced red and orange peppers or a mix of peppers and diced courgettes.

Smoked mackerel fishcake roll

Meaty burgers are always popular but if, like many of our café customers, you are trying to reduce the amount of meat that you eat then this makes a great alternative.

Serves 4
Prep 30 minutes
Cook 27 minutes

FISHCAKES
500g/1lb 2oz potatoes, peeled, cut into chunks
250g/9oz smoked mackerel fillets, skinned
1 tbsp mayonnaise
1 egg yolk
15g/½oz fresh parsley, finely chopped
100g/3½oz breadcrumbs
Salt and pepper
3 tbsp vegetable oil

TO FINISH
4 soft bread rolls
115g/4oz mayonnaise
60g/2¼oz gherkins, drained, chopped
20g/¾oz rocket
Lemon wedges to serve, optional

Add the potatoes to a saucepan of boiling water and cook for 15 minutes until tender. Drain well and steam dry in the pan, then mash the potatoes lightly, leaving some chunks. Set aside and leave to cool.

Flake the mackerel into small pieces with two forks. Mix the mayonnaise and egg into the mashed potato. Fold in the mackerel, chopped parsley, 50g/1¾oz breadcrumbs and a little salt and pepper until evenly mixed.

Divide the mixture into four then shape into round cakes about 10cm/4 inches in diameter on a chopping board.

Put the remaining breadcrumbs on a plate, then press each fishcake into the crumbs until both sides are coated. Chill until ready to cook.

Preheat the oven to 180°C/350°F/gas mark 4 and line a roasting tin with non-stick baking paper. Add the oil to a large frying pan, add the fishcakes and fry for 1 minute on each side or until golden brown. Lift out of the pan, transfer to the lined roasting tin and bake in the oven for 10 minutes until piping hot.

Cut the bread rolls in half. Mix the mayonnaise with the chopped gherkins and a little pepper. Spread over each roll half. Arrange the rocket leaves on the bottom half of the rolls, top each with a fishcake, squeeze with a little lemon juice if liked, then add the roll tops. Serve immediately with a little extra salad if liked.

COOK'S TIP The fishcakes can be made up earlier in the day or the day before if that suits you better. Cover with clingfilm and keep in the fridge.

Panzanella

This chunky, colourful, peasant-style salad is just bursting with flavour. What could be nicer than a bowl of this enjoyed in the garden with some homemade lemonade or a glass of mint tea?

Serves 4
Prep 20 minutes
Cook 10–20 minutes

1 red pepper, quartered, cored, deseeded
1 yellow pepper, quartered, cored, deseeded
125g/4½oz day-old rustic bread, torn into pieces
1 tbsp vegetable oil
Salt and pepper
½ cucumber, deseeded, sliced
250g/9oz tomatoes, cut into chunks
½ small red onion, thinly sliced
10g/¼oz fresh basil, torn into pieces, small leaves left whole
15g/½oz drained capers

DRESSING
2 tbsp extra virgin rapeseed oil
2 tsp white wine vinegar
1 garlic clove, finely chopped
½ tsp wholegrain mustard

Preheat the grill. Line the base of the grill pan with foil then arrange the pepper quarters skin-side uppermost. Grill for 5–10 minutes until the skins have blackened and blistered. Wrap the foil around the peppers and leave to cool.

Preheat the oven to 190°C/375°F/gas mark 5. Arrange the bread in an even layer in a roasting tin, drizzle with the oil and season with a little salt and pepper then toss together. Bake in the oven for 5–10 minutes, turning once, until crisp and golden. Leave to cool.

Add the cucumber, tomatoes, onion, basil and capers to a salad bowl and toss together. Scrape the skins from the peppers then cut into chunks and add to the salad with any juices.

Fork the dressing ingredients together with a little salt and pepper then pour over the salad. Add the bread, toss gently together and leave to stand for 30 minutes before serving.

COOK'S TIP The salad components can all be prepared in advance – just don't add the bread until 30 minutes before serving or it will go too soft.

Cod, bbq lettuce, honey & ginger noodles

This delicious Thai-inspired noodle dish can be prepared in less time than it would take to dash out for a takeaway. Light, fresh and full of flavour, this is comfort food, summer style.

Serves 4
Prep 15 minutes
Cook 10 minutes

200g/7oz rice noodles
½ bunch spring onions, cut
    into 4cm/1½inch lengths
    then into matchstick strips

SAUCE
3 tbsp white wine vinegar
120ml/4fl oz extra virgin
    rapeseed oil
2 tsp runny honey
15g/½oz root ginger, peeled,
    finely chopped
1 red chilli, halved, deseeded,
    finely chopped
Salt and pepper

TO FINISH
4 x 140g/5oz portions of cod,
    skinned
4 tsp sesame seeds
2 little gem lettuces, trimmed,
    halved

Cook the noodles as the pack directs, drain and refresh with cold water, then drain again and set aside.

Add all the sauce ingredients to a liquidiser and blend until smooth or add the ingredients to a jam jar, screw on the lid and shake for a slightly coarser sauce.

Season the fish portions with salt and pepper and steam for 5 minutes or until the fish can be broken into clear white flakes.

Heat a non-stick frying pan – no need for oil – add the sesame seeds and toast for a few minutes until golden brown. Scoop out of the pan and reserve. Wipe the pan with kitchen towel, reheat then add the lettuce halves, cut-side downwards and cook for 1 minute on each side until lightly coloured. Take out of the pan, reheat the noodles with a little of the sauce and the spring onions.

Spoon the noodles onto plates, arrange the cod on top, sprinkle with the sesame seeds and add the lettuce to one side. Drizzle over the remaining sauce and serve.

COOK'S TIP If you are a fan of fresh coriander, add a sprinkling of finely chopped leaves to the noodles when reheating.

Chicken & basil broth

A lighter, fresher twist on a casserole, packed with all the flavours of the Mediterranean.

Serves 4
Prep 20 minutes
Cook 1 hour

1 tbsp vegetable oil
100g/3½oz onions, roughly chopped
300g/10½oz boneless, skinless chicken thighs, cut into chunks
85ml/3fl oz red wine
4 tsp tomato purée
345ml/12fl oz chicken stock
½ red pepper, cored, deseeded, roughly chopped
85g/3oz celery, roughly chopped
170g/6oz potatoes, roughly chopped
100g/3½oz carrots, roughly chopped
½ tsp dried mixed herbs
Salt and pepper
400g/14oz can chickpeas, drained, rinsed with cold water and drained again
200g/7oz tomatoes, roughly chopped
20g/¾oz fresh basil, finely chopped

TO FINISH
3 tbsp extra virgin rapeseed oil
1 tsp white wine vinegar
½ tsp caster sugar

Heat the oil in a saucepan, add the onion and fry over a medium heat for 5 minutes, stirring until softened. Add the chicken and fry for 5 more minutes until the chicken is sealed.

Add the red wine and tomato purée and stir well to deglaze the pan then pour in the stock. Add the peppers, celery, potatoes, carrots, dried herbs and a little salt and pepper. Bring to the boil, stirring, then cover and simmer for 30 minutes, stirring from time to time until the chicken and vegetables are cooked through.

Add the chickpeas to the saucepan with the fresh tomatoes and half the basil. Simmer gently for 20 minutes.

Meanwhile, warm the rapeseed oil in a small saucepan with the remaining chopped basil, vinegar, sugar and a little salt and pepper, then set aside.

Ladle the chicken and basil broth into bowls, drizzle with the basil oil and serve with warm olive or plain ciabatta bread.

COOK'S TIP This broth freezes well either in one large lidded plastic container or smaller individual ones. Add the basil oil after reheating.

Vietnamese chicken salad

Convert those members of the family who aren't keen on salad with this rice noodle salad packed with fresh mint, cucumber and pineapple, sprinkled with a caramelised chilli nut topping.

Serves 4
Prep 20 minutes
Cook 5 minutes

4 tsp sweet chilli sauce
1 small lime, juice only
½ tsp dried chilli flakes
¼ tsp ground ginger
1 tsp soft light brown sugar
½ cucumber, deseeded, thinly sliced
4 spring onions, thinly sliced
3 tbsp fresh chopped mint
3 tbsp fresh chopped coriander
200g/7oz white cabbage, finely shredded
115g/4oz thin rice noodles, cooked as pack instructions, drained
1 slice of fresh pineapple, about 70g/2½oz, peeled, cored, diced

TOPPING
50g/1¾oz mixed chopped nuts
4 tsp caster sugar
¼ tsp paprika
1 garlic clove, finely chopped
¼ tsp dried chilli flakes
200g/7oz cooked chicken breast, torn into shreds

Mix together the sweet chilli sauce, lime juice, chilli flakes, ginger and sugar and set the dressing aside.

Add the cucumber, spring onions and herbs to a large bowl and stir together. Add the white cabbage, cooked drained noodles and pineapple and mix together.

Add the chopped nuts to a dry frying pan and fry over a medium heat until golden, add the sugar, paprika, garlic and chilli flakes and continue to stir until the sugar has dissolved and caramelised. Turn onto a plate and leave to cool.

Pour the chilli dressing over the noodle mixture, add the shredded chicken and toss together. Spoon into serving bowls and sprinkle with some of the nuts.

COOK'S TIP Don't add the chilli dressing until just before serving the salad so that the cucumber stays crunchy.

If you had a roast chicken the day before, make the most of the remaining meat in this salad. Or for a fish version you might like to try with some defrosted cooked prawns or some cooked, flaked salmon instead.

Picnic pie with relish

At the National Trust we are well known for our lovely properties to visit, but you can also rent holiday cottages in the most beautiful locations. If you are planning a trip away with friends or family, this pie would make a very welcome picnic lunch to take with you and enjoy when you arrive, with leftovers for the next day too.

Cuts into 12 slices
Prep 50 minutes
Cook 1¾ hours

PASTRY
500g/1lb 2oz plain flour
185g/6½oz lard, diced
60g/2¼oz butter, diced
Salt and pepper
2 eggs, beaten
1–2 tbsp water

FILLING
150g/5½oz stuffing mix
250g/9oz onions, finely
    chopped
900g/2lb pork sausagemeat
15g/½oz thyme, leaves
    stripped from stems,
    chopped
250g/9oz tart dessert apples,
    cored, sliced
250g/9oz or 2 small boneless
    skinless chicken breasts,
    thinly sliced
250g/9oz onion chutney
1 egg, beaten, to glaze

Preheat the oven to 190°C/375°F/gas mark 5. Add the flour, lard, butter and a little salt and pepper to the bowl of your mixer or food processor and rub in the fat until it resembles fine crumbs. Add the egg and enough water to bring together to form a smooth dough. Reserve one third of the pastry for the pie lid and wrap in clingfilm. Chill the pastry for 30 minutes.

Lightly knead the rest of the pastry then roll out on a floured surface to a large circle about 35cm/14 inches in diameter. Fold the pastry into four then lift up and put inside a 23cm/9 inch springclip tin. With floured hands, open out the pastry and ease over the base and up the sides so that the pastry overhangs the top of the tin by at least 2cm/¾ inch.

Add the stuffing mix to a mixing bowl and stir in enough boiling water to make a thick stuffing, according to the pack instructions. Stir in the onions and leave to cool.

Mix the sausagemeat in a second bowl with two thirds of the chopped thyme, salt and pepper.

Spoon the stuffing mix over the base of the pie and press gently into an even layer, then add half the sausagemeat mix and press this into an even layer. Arrange the apple slices on top and sprinkle with the remaining thyme. Cover with the chicken slices, then spoon over the chutney. Lastly top with the remaining sausagemeat and press gently together.

Continued overleaf

RELISH

10g/¼oz cornflour

6 tbsp red wine

50g/1¾oz caster sugar

100g/3½oz gherkins, drained, roughly chopped

100g/3½oz frozen silverskin onions, defrosted, roughly chopped

100g/3½oz frozen sweetcorn

100g/3½oz cauliflower, cut into small florets, core discarded

Brush the top edge of the pastry with beaten egg, Roll the remaining pastry out a little larger than the tin, lift over a rolling pin and position on top of the pie. Press the edges together well, trim off the excess pastry and crimp the top edge to seal well. Make a hole in the centre of the pie and decorate with leaves cut from the pastry trimmings. Glaze the top of the pie with beaten egg.

Put the tin on a baking sheet and cook for 15 minutes, then reduce the temperature to 160°/325°F/gas mark 3 for a further 90 minutes or until a meat thermometer reads 75°C/170°F in the centre of the pie. Remove from the oven and leave to cool in the tin for 30 minutes, then loosen the sides of the pie with a palette knife and unclip the tin but do not remove. When completely cold, cover with foil and chill in the fridge for 3–4 hours, or overnight if you can.

Meanwhile, make the relish by mixing the cornflour to a smooth paste with 1 tablespoon of the vinegar. Add the remaining vinegar to a saucepan with the sugar and bring to the boil. Stir in the cornflour paste and cook, stirring until thickened. Add the chopped vegetables and salt and pepper to taste. Leave to cool, then pack into a cliptop jar or plastic container. This will keep in the fridge in a cliptop jar for up to a week.

Loosen the edge of the pie again then remove the tin sides, run a palette knife under the pie and transfer to a chopping board.

Cut into wedges and serve with spoonfuls of the relish and a mixed salad.

COOK'S TIP Pickled silverskin onions, rinsed and drained, can be used in place of the frozen onions.

Seasonal goat's cheese gnocchi

These small Italian potato dumplings can be shaped and cooked earlier in the day, then reheated in a frying pan with a little rapeseed oil until golden. Serve on a bed of summery vegetables bathed in a light, creamy sauce and topped with dainty pea shoots – perfect served with a glass of chilled white wine.

Serves 4
Prep 40 minutes
Cook 11 minutes

GNOCCHI
200g/7oz potatoes, peeled,
   boiled and mashed
40g/1½oz goat's cheese
1 egg yolk
60g/2¼oz plain flour
½ tsp dried oregano
Salt and pepper

SAUCE
30g/1oz butter
2 tbsp plain flour
4 tbsp white wine
200ml/7fl vegetable stock
4 tbsp double cream

TO SERVE
3 tbsp cold pressed
   rapeseed oil
125g/4½oz button
   mushrooms, quartered
140g/5oz leeks, thinly
   shredded
125g/4½oz mangetout
15g/½oz flat-leaf parsley,
   finely chopped
40g/1½oz pea shoots

Add the mashed potato to a bowl, crumble in the goat's cheese, add the egg yolk, flour and oregano then season with salt and pepper. Mix together with a spoon at first, then mould together into a ball with your hands making sure it is well mixed.

Divide the dough into four pieces then roll each piece into a rope shape on a lightly floured surface until about 1cm/½ inch in diameter. Cut into pieces the width of your thumb.

Half fill a large saucepan with water, bring to the boil then gradually drop about one third of the gnocchi, a few pieces at a time, into the water. They will sink at first and then float to the surface when they are cooked, about 3 minutes. Scoop out of the pan with a draining spoon and add to a bowl of chilled water to cool quickly. Continue cooking the gnocchi in batches until you've used up all the dough.

To make the sauce, heat the butter in a small saucepan, stir in the flour then mix in the wine until you have a smooth paste. Gradually stir in the stock and heat, still stirring, until the sauce is smooth and thickened. Stir in the cream then add salt and pepper to taste.

Heat a little oil in a frying pan, add the mushrooms and fry for a few minutes until lightly coloured. Steam the leeks and mangetout for 2 minutes, then add to the frying pan along with the parsley. Stir together then stir into the sauce and reheat the sauce if needed.

Drain the gnocchi well in a colander. Wipe the frying pan clean with kitchen towel then heat a little oil in the pan. Add the gnocchi and fry, gently stirring until reheated and lightly coloured.

Spoon the vegetables and sauce into serving bowls, top with the lightly fried gnocchi, some pea shoots and a drizzle of oil and serve immediately.

Chicken, pea & mint crush with lemon dressing

Roast chicken is the ultimate in comfort food. This quick summery version serves the chicken on a bed of puréed peas mixed with fresh mint and spring onion, with a fresh-tasting lemon-parsley dressing over baby new potatoes.

Serves 4
Prep 20 minutes
Cook 20 minutes

500g/1lb 2oz baby new
   potatoes, scrubbed, halved
   or left whole depending on
   size
4 chicken supremes or chicken
   breasts with skin on, each
   about 170g/6oz
Salt and pepper
1 tbsp vegetable oil
400g/14oz fresh podded or
   frozen peas
15g/½oz fresh mint
2 spring onions

DRESSING
100ml/3½fl oz extra virgin
   rapeseed oil
4 tbsp finely chopped fresh
   parsley
½ lemon, grated zest and
   juice
Salt and pepper

Preheat the oven to 180°C/350°F/gas mark 4.

Add the potatoes to a saucepan of boiling water and simmer for about 15 minutes until tender.

Meanwhile, season the chicken breasts with a little salt and pepper. Heat the oil in a large frying pan then fry the chicken over a high heat for 5 minutes, turning once until browned on both sides. Transfer to a roasting tin, cover with foil and bake in the oven for 15 minutes until cooked through and the juices run clear when the centre of one of the breasts is pierced with a knife. If you have a meat thermometer it should read 75°C/170°C.

Bring a second pan of water to the boil and add the peas. Bring back to the boil, then take off the heat and leave to stand for 5 minutes before draining.

Add the drained peas to a food processor with the mint and spring onions and blend to a rough-textured purée. Spoon back into the saucepan, cover and keep warm.

To make the dressing, whisk the oil, parsley, lemon zest and juice together in a bowl then season with a little salt and pepper.

Spoon one quarter of the peas slightly offset on each of four serving plates. Serve the chicken supremes whole, or cut the chicken breasts into thick slices and fan out on top of the peas. Spoon the potatoes to the side then drizzle the potatoes and chicken with the parsley and lemon dressing.

Pepper, tomato & cheese quiche

Not everyone feels confident making pastry but this sweet potato rosti-style case is easy to make and gluten-free. Filled with a light, herby cheese custard flecked with roasted red pepper and cherry tomatoes.

Serves 6–8
Prep 30 minutes
Cook 45–50 minutes

QUICHE CASE
Little oil for greasing
340g/12oz sweet potato, peeled, grated
1 egg, beaten
50g/1¾oz cheddar cheese, grated
¼ tsp dried chilli flakes
Salt and pepper

FILLING
1 red pepper, halved, cored, deseeded, roasted (see page 66), skinned and chopped
70g/2½oz spring onions, finely chopped
170g/6oz cherry tomatoes, halved
4 tbsp fresh chopped parsley
5 eggs
200ml/7fl oz milk
55ml/2 fl oz double cream
100g/3½oz cheddar cheese, grated

Preheat the oven to 180°C/350°F/gas mark 4. Lightly brush the base and sides of a loose-bottomed 23cm/9 inch sandwich tin with a little oil. Put the sweet potato into a sieve and squeeze out as much liquid as you can. Add to a bowl and mix in the egg, cheese, chilli flakes and a little salt and pepper.

Spoon the mixture into the oiled tin and press into an even layer over the base and up the sides with the back of a spoon, keep a little mixture back and use to patch any holes after baking.

Bake the tart case in the oven for about 15 minutes until the potato is set and just beginning to crisp around the edges. Check for any holes and patch with the reserved mixture.

Add the diced roasted pepper to a bowl with the spring onions, tomatoes and parsley and mix well. Add the eggs, milk and cream to a separate bowl and whisk together, then mix in the cheese and a little salt and pepper.

Add the pepper mix to the custard, stir well then spoon into the tart case. Bake at 160°C/325°F/gas mark 3 for about 35 minutes until the top is golden with a slight wobble still in the centre. Leave to cool in the tin then loosen the tart edge with a palette knife and remove from the tin. Cut into wedges and serve with new potatoes, coleslaw and a leafy salad.

COOK'S TIP If you don't have a sandwich tin the right size you can use the same size spring-form tin, press the sweet potato only two thirds of the way up the sides of the tin so that the quiche case will be 4cm/1½ inch deep.

DOG ROSE   *Rosa canina*

Family ROSACEAE   In hedges and copses throughout Britain the Dog Rose may be found. It is the largest of the British wild roses.

The rootstock is woody, frequently producing suckers, from which rise the long arching branches covered with stout and sharp hooks, often reaching a length of six or eight feet, and forming a bush of considerable size.

The leaves are broken up into five or seven sharply-toothed leaflets.

The sweet-scented pink or white flowers are borne solitary or three or four together, at the ends of the branches, the large elliptical bracts. The developed leaves forming elliptical bracts. The sepals are five in number, when pinnate, and turned towards the stem, when the flower is open. There are five notched petals and many stamens. The styles are free and hairy. The ovary is sunk in the calyx, which changes to the pitcher-shaped scarlet fruits, known as "hips," in which are the hairy achenes.

The flowering period extends from June to August.

98

Open ravioli with egg & spinach cream sauce

Light, pretty and elegant, this main course captures the essence of summer. If you like eggs Benedict you will love this, and the creamy wine sauce is much easier to make than hollandaise and just as lovely.

Serves 4
Prep 20 minutes
Cook 16–23 minutes

400ml/14fl oz white wine
1 small bay leaf
400ml/200ml double cream
Salt and pepper
2 tbsp fresh chopped parsley
1 tsp vegetable oil
8 dried lasagne sheets
15g/½oz butter
400g/14oz baby leaf spinach
4–8 eggs
1 tsp white wine vinegar
85g/3oz smoked cheddar,
    thinly sliced
200g/7oz tomatoes, quartered,
    deseeded, diced
2 tbsp fresh chopped chives

Pour the wine into a saucepan, add the bay leaf and boil over a medium heat for about 5 minutes until reduced by half. Add the cream and a little salt and pepper and cook for 2–3 minutes until thick. Remove the bay leaf and stir in the parsley. Set aside.

Bring a large saucepan of water to the boil, add the oil and a little salt then the lasagne sheets and cook for 5–8 minutes until just tender. Drain into a colander.

Melt the butter in a large frying pan, add the spinach and a little salt and pepper then stir fry for 2–3 minutes until just wilted and bright green. Cover with a lid and set aside.

Bring a medium saucepan of water to the boil, add the vinegar and a little salt then gradually drop four eggs into the water and cook over a gentle simmer for 4–5 minutes until the eggs are just set. If serving two eggs per portion, cook in two batches.

Arrange a sheet of lasagne in the base of each of four shallow bowls, folding the sheets to add interest. Reheat the spinach if needed, spoon over the pasta, then add one or two drained eggs to each bowl. Top with the cheese then a second folded sheet of pasta.

Warm the sauce then spoon over the top, garnish with the chopped tomatoes, chives and a little black pepper and serve immediately.

COOK'S TIP If you are feeling extra hungry, allow two poached eggs per portion rather than one.

Frozen chopped spinach can be used if preferred, just make sure to press out the liquid in a sieve once thawed, and warm through in the frying pan as above.

Mixed bean chilli

This easy meat-free chilli can be served with rice or in bowls with warm bread, or dressed up with spoonfuls of mashed avocado mixed with lime juice and chopped coriander, or topped with tortilla chips and grated cheese. Any leftovers can be spooned over a microwave jacket potato for a speedy lunch the next day.

Serves 4
Prep 20 minutes
Cook 31 minutes

1 tbsp vegetable oil
300g/10½oz onions, chopped
2 garlic cloves, finely chopped
1 tsp dried chilli flakes
½ tsp ground cumin
½ tsp ground coriander
1 tsp sweet smoked paprika
½ tsp dried oregano
4 tsp tomato purée
4 tbsp red wine
1 tbsp light brown sugar
450g/1lb tomatoes, chopped
150ml/¼pt vegetable stock
400g/14oz can 5-bean mix in
    water, drained
400g/14oz can red kidney
    beans in water, drained
2 tbsp fresh chopped
    coriander, optional
Salt and pepper

Heat the oil in a saucepan, add the onion and garlic and fry for 10 minutes, stirring from time to time until lightly browned.

Stir in the chilli flakes, ground spices and oregano and cook for 1 minute. Stir in the tomato purée, wine and sugar and cook gently for 5 minutes, stirring frequently.

Add the tomatoes and stock, stir well and bring to the boil then add the drained beans. Cover and simmer for 15 minutes, stirring from time to time and adding a little extra stock or water if needed, until the tomatoes are soft and saucy.

Stir in the chopped coriander, if using, and salt and pepper to taste. Spoon into bowls and serve with warm bread or garlic bread.

COOK'S TIP This freezes well in individual portions in plastic containers. Microwave in the freezer container and serve for a speedy lunch or supper.

If you don't like your chilli too hot then reduce the amount of dried chilli flakes down to ½ teaspoon.

Tandoori chicken

You don't need a special tandoor oven for this, just a traditional ovenproof dish. Prepare and marinate the chicken the night before for the best flavour, then bake when you get home from work. Spatchcocking, or cutting and flattening, the chicken means that it cooks in half the time.

Serves 4
Prep 35 minutes
Marinate overnight
Cook 40–45 minutes

1 small 1.2kg/2.6lb oven-ready
    chicken
5 cardamom pods
4 tsp tikka curry paste
70g/2½oz Greek-style natural
    yogurt
1 tsp sweet smoked paprika
4 tortilla wraps

SLAW
100g/3½oz green cabbage,
    finely shredded
100g/3½oz fennel, finely
    shredded
100g/3½oz carrots, grated
2 spring onions, finely
    chopped
2 tbsp fresh chopped parsley
½ lime, grated zest and juice
4 tsp sesame oil

TO SERVE
115g/4oz Greek-style natural
    yogurt
2 tbsp fresh chopped mint
Salt and pepper

First spatchcock the chicken, put the chicken breast-side down on a chopping board then, using poultry shears or a strong pair of kitchen scissors, cut down each side of the spine and remove it. Cut off the wing tips and the ends of the drumsticks.

Turn the chicken over, put into a large shallow china dish and open out flat, pressing the breasts down with the palm of your hand. Score the skin and flesh all over with a small sharp knife.

Flatten the cardamom pods with the back of a knife then peel away the outer green casing. Crush the tiny black seeds in a pestle and mortar or in a cup with the end of a rolling pin. Add the ground seeds to a small bowl with the tikka paste, yogurt and paprika and stir together. Spoon all over the chicken, massaging into the meat with fingertips or the back of a spoon. Cover with clingfilm and marinate in the fridge overnight.

Next day, preheat the oven to 200°C/400°F/gas mark 6. Remove the clingfilm and leave the chicken in the dish if ovenproof or transfer to a roasting tin. Roast for 10 minutes, then reduce the heat to 180°C/350°F/gas mark 4 for 30–35 minutes until the chicken is browned and thoroughly cooked or a meat thermometer inserted into the thickest part of the breast and leg reads 75°C/170°F. Or test by piercing the thickest part of the one of the legs with a small knife; the juices should run clear. If not, cook for an extra 10–15 minutes.

Meanwhile, mix all the slaw ingredients together in a bowl. Spoon the yogurt into a second smaller bowl and stir in the chopped mint and a little salt and pepper.

When ready to serve, cut the chicken into pieces and arrange on serving plates with spoonfuls of the slaw, minted yogurt and warmed tortillas, cut into quarters.

Italian sausage stew

We should all be eating more vegetables, and this easy, colourful supper fits the bill. Serve in bowls with some bread to mop up the juices or try with some pasta or rice if preferred.

Serves 4
Prep 15 minutes
Cook 20 minutes

6 large pork sausages
1 tbsp vegetable oil
200g/7oz red onion, chopped
1 yellow pepper, deseeded, cut
    into large dice
1 red pepper, deseeded, cut
    into large dice
2 garlic cloves, finely chopped
1 bay leaf
2 stems fresh thyme, leaves
    stripped from stems
70g/2½oz tomato purée
450g/1lb tomatoes, cut into
    quarters
4 tbsp red wine
345ml/12fl oz chicken or
    vegetable stock
Salt and pepper
2 tbsp fresh chopped parsley
    to garnish

Slit the sausages along their length and peel away the skins, then cut into thick slices. Heat the oil in a large frying pan, add the sausage pieces and fry over a medium heat for 5 minutes, stirring until browned all over.

Add the red onion, peppers, garlic, bay leaf and thyme and fry for 5 minutes.

Mix in the tomato paste, then add the quartered tomatoes and red wine. Cook, stirring, for a minute or two to deglaze the bottom of the pan, then pour in the stock to just cover everything. Season with a little salt and pepper. Bring to the boil, then reduce the heat and simmer uncovered for about 10 minutes until the tomatoes are softened but still hold their shape and the sauce has reduced a little.

Discard the bay leaf. Sprinkle with the parsley, then ladle into bowls and serve with warm bread and butter.

COOK'S TIP You could also use 285g/10oz pork sausagemeat for this recipe, cut into pieces that are 20g/¾oz and fried as above.

Raspberry & white chocolate muffins

Much as we all love chocolate, it can get pretty messy on a picnic. Adding white chocolate chips and juicy raspberries to vanilla muffins is the best of both worlds, and without the sticky fingers.

Makes 12
Prep 15 minutes
Cook 20–25 minutes

500g/1lb 2oz plain flour
250g/9oz caster sugar
1½ tsp baking powder
2 tsp bicarbonate of soda
300ml/½ pt milk
3 eggs
120ml/4fl oz vegetable oil
1 tbsp vanilla extract

TO FINISH
125g/4½ oz white chocolate
　 drops
150g/5½ oz raspberries

Preheat the oven to 180°C/350°F/gas mark 4. Line a 12-hole deep muffin tin with tulip-shaped paper muffin cases.

Place all the dry ingredients into a large bowl and stir together.

Add all the wet ingredients to a second bowl and whisk together until smooth.

Add the wet ingredients to the dry and whisk together until partially mixed. Add the chocolate and raspberries and stir together until just mixed.

Divide between the muffin cases and bake for 20–25 minutes until well risen and golden brown or until a skewer comes out cleanly when inserted into the centre of one of the muffins.

Remove from the tin and leave to cool on a wire rack.

COOK'S TIP These are generous-sized muffins so make sure to use large tulip paper cases rather than the shallower flat-topped paper cases.

Frozen raspberries can also be used, just defrost for 20 minutes or so to partially thaw before adding to the muffin mix.

Blueberry & thyme cheesecake slice

Many of our kitchen gardens also have wonderful herb gardens. Herbs needn't just be in savoury dishes but sweet too, where they add a gentle perfume. If you have lemon thyme, do try using it here.

Cuts into 10–12 slices
Prep 30 minutes
Cook 35–40 minutes

SPONGE BASE
140g/5oz soft margarine
50g/1¾oz soft light brown sugar
85g/3oz caster sugar
3 eggs
170g/6oz gluten-free self-raising flour
½ tsp gluten-free baking powder

CHEESECAKE
150g/5½oz full fat cream cheese
½ lemon, grated zest only
1 egg, beaten
40g/1½oz caster sugar
½ tsp vanilla extract
100g/3½oz blueberries
1 tsp fresh thyme leaves

Preheat the oven to 180°C/350°F/gas mark 4. Line a 18 x 28 x 4cm/ 7 x 11 x 1½ inch shallow rectangular cake tin with a large piece of non-stick baking paper, snipping the paper diagonally into the corners of the tin and pressing the paper down so that the base and sides are lined.

To make the sponge base, add the margarine, sugars, eggs, flour and baking powder to the bowl of your mixer and beat slowly until roughly mixed, then increase the speed and beat until light and fluffy.

Spoon the sponge mixture into the lined tin and spread into an even thicknesss.

To make the cheesecake, add the cream cheese, lemon zest, egg, sugar and vanilla to a bowl and beat until smooth. Spoon over the sponge layer to make a thin, even layer.

Scatter the blueberries and thyme leaves on top and bake for 35–40 minutes until well risen, golden brown and the cheesecake is beginning to crack slightly. A skewer will come out cleanly when inserted into the centre of the cake.

Leave to cool slightly in the tin then lift the cake out holding the paper and cool completely on a wire rack. Cut into bars and lift off the paper to serve.

Chocolate éclairs

Lord Preston, owner of Nunnington Hall in North Yorkshire, was Ambassador to the Palace of Versailles and as tribute to his time in such a prestigious position the chefs here have developed the recipe for these elegant éclairs. I like to imagine them served on the beautiful French porcelain displayed in the Drawing Room.

Makes 14
Prep 30 minutes
Cook 18–20 minutess

CHOUX PASTRY
Little butter for greasing
150ml/¼ pt water
55g/2oz unsalted butter, diced
1 tsp caster sugar
70g/2½ oz plain flour
Pinch sea salt
2 eggs, beaten

FILLING
225ml/8fl oz double cream

ICING
55g/2oz dark chocolate, chopped
1 tsp butter
2 tbsp water
85g/3oz icing sugar, sifted

To make the choux pastry, preheat the oven to 200°C/400°F/gas mark 6. Lightly grease a large baking sheet with a little butter.

Add the water, butter and sugar to a medium saucepan and heat gently until the butter has melted. Bring to the boil, take the pan off the heat, sieve in the flour and salt and then quickly return to a high heat and stir constantly for 2 minutes until the mixture thickens and forms a smooth ball that leaves the sides of the saucepan cleanly. Stand the saucepan in cold water to cool for 20 minutes.

Gradually add the beaten eggs, mixing well with a wooden spoon or electric mixer until smooth.

Spoon the choux paste into a large piping bag fitted with a 1cm/½ inch plain tube. Pipe 7½cm/3 inch lengths onto the greased baking sheet. Bake for 18–20 minutes until well risen and crisp.

Slit down one side of each éclair with a sharp knife to allow the steam to escape then transfer to a wire rack and leave to cool.

Lightly whip the cream in a bowl until it forms soft swirls. Spoon into a piping bag fitted with a slightly smaller tube, then pipe into the éclairs.

Set a heatproof bowl over a saucepan of gently simmering water so that the bottom of the bowl doesn't touch the water. Add the chocolate, butter and water to the bowl and heat gently, stirring occasionally until the chocolate has melted.

Stir in the sieved sugar a little at a time until smooth and glossy.

Spoon the chocolate icing over the top of the éclairs then smooth with a small palette knife. Leave in a cool place to set.

Courgette, lemon & thyme sponge

More and more of our visitors to the cafés are requesting gluten-free cakes. This light, fluffy, summery cake is always a hit when on the menu and enjoyed by everyone, not just those on special diets. Courgette and thyme might seem like unusual ingredients to add to a cake, but the courgette adds moistness and the thyme a summery fragrance – if you can get lemon thyme, this is even better.

Cuts into 8 slices
Prep 40 minutes
Cook 25 minutes

285g/10oz gluten-free self-
    raising flour
¾ tsp gluten-free baking
    powder
¾ tsp bicarbonate of soda
¾ tsp xanthan gum
250g/9oz butter or soft
    margarine
200g/7oz caster sugar
5 eggs
1 lemon, grated zest and juice
225g/8oz courgette, coarsely
    grated
2 tbsp thyme leaves

CANDIED COURGETTE
55g/2oz caster sugar
1 lemon, grated zest and juice
55g/2oz courgette, cut into
    matchstick strips
1 tsp thyme leaves

FILLING
70g/2½oz butter or soft
    margarine
100g/3½oz icing sugar
2 tbsp runny honey

Preheat the oven to 160°C/325°F/gas mark 3. Grease and base line two 20cm/8 inch loose-bottomed sandwich tins.

Add the flour, baking powder, bicarbonate of soda and xanthan gum to a bowl and stir together.

Cream the soft margarine and sugar in a bowl with an electric mixer until light and fluffy. Add the eggs, one at a time, beating well after each addition and spooning in a little of the flour mix to stop the mixture from separating.

Gradually mix in the remaining flour then the lemon zest and juice. Pat the courgettes dry with kitchen paper, then fold into the cake mixture with the thyme leaves. Divide the cake mixture between the two tins and level the top. Bake for about 25 minutes until well risen and golden and a skewer comes out of the centre cleanly.

Leave to cool in the tins for 5 minutes, then loosen the edge and turn out onto a cooling rack.

To make the candied courgette, line a baking sheet with non-stick paper. Add the sugar and lemon juice to a saucepan and bring to the boil, stirring until the sugar has dissolved. Add the lemon zest, courgette and thyme and boil for 2 minutes until softened and the mixture is syrupy. Spoon over the baking sheet and leave to cool.

Add all the filling ingredients to a mixer bowl or food processor and beat until light and fluffy. Remove the lining paper from the cakes. Put one cake onto a serving plate, spread with the filling then top with the second cake and press together lightly. Spoon the candied courgettes on top. Cut into slices to serve.

Raspberry rippled cheesecake cake

This delicious cake really has the wow factor. Rather than taking a bottle of wine to a summer barbecue party, impress friends and family by taking this instead.

Cuts into 12 slices
Prep 45 minutes
Cook 1¼ hours–1 hour 20
  minutes

340g/12oz soft margarine
300g/10½oz caster sugar
7 eggs
340g/12oz self-raising flour
1 tsp baking powder
150g/5oz frozen raspberries

FOR THE CHEESECAKE
125g/4½oz Greek-style yogurt
370g/13oz full fat cream
  cheese
1 egg
125g/4½oz honey

TO FINISH
100g/3½oz seedless raspberry
  jam
Few extra raspberries,
  defrosted if frozen, optional
Little sifted icing sugar,
  optional

Preheat the oven to 160°C/325°F/gas mark 3. Grease with a little oil and base line two 23cm/9 inch loose-bottomed sandwich tins.

Add the margarine and sugar to the bowl of your mixer and cream together until light and fluffy. Gradually beat in the eggs, one at a time, adding a spoonful of flour and beating well between each addition until smooth.

Gradually mix in the remaining flour and baking powder. Cut half the raspberries in half, then add to the cake mix with the whole raspberries and gently fold together. Divide the cake mixture between the two tins and spread the tops level.

Bake for 35–40 minutes until the cakes are well risen, golden brown and a skewer comes out cleanly when inserted into the centre. Leave to cool, then turn out of the tins. Turn the oven down to 150°C/350°F/gas mark 2.

Wash one of the tins, dry, oil and line the base with fresh non-stick baking paper. Place all the cheesecake ingredients into the bowl of your mixer and beat until smooth. Pour into the lined tin and bake for 40 minutes until set with a slight wobble in the centre. Take out of the oven and leave to cool. Chill for 2–3 hours in the fridge until set firm.

Peel the lining paper off the cakes. Put one of the cakes top-down on a cake plate and spread with half the raspberry jam. Remove the cheesecake from the tin but keep it on the tin base. Place the cheesecake layer top-down on the jam. Remove the tin base and lining paper from the cheesecake. Spread the remaining jam over the base of the other cake then sandwich on top of the cheesecake layer – this is the tricky bit! Sprinkle with extra raspberries, if liked, and dust lightly with icing sugar. Cut into slices to serve.

Summer fruit panna cotta

Silky smooth, with just a hint of vanilla, these softly set desserts lift summer strawberries and cream to another level.

Serves 4
Prep 15 minutes
Cook 10 minutes
Chill 4 hours

200g/7oz summer berries:
   a mix of strawberries,
   raspberries and blueberries,
   if using strawberries, hull
   and quarter or roughly chop
   if large.
2 tbsp water
2 sheets gelatine
300ml/½pt double cream
100ml/3½fl oz milk
60g/2¼oz caster sugar
1 tsp vanilla extract

TO FINISH
4 tsp raspberry jam
Few extra raspberries,
   defrosted if frozen, optional
Little sifted icing sugar,
   optional

Add half the fruit to a small saucepan with 2 tablespoons of water, gently warm together for 5 minutes until the juices just begin to run. Cool.

Put the gelatine in a shallow dish, cover with cold water and leave to soften for 5 minutes.

Warm the cream, milk and sugar in a saucepan, stirring all the time until the sugar has dissolved, then bring just to the boil. Take off the heat, drain the gelatine, add the softened sheets to the cream mix with the vanilla and stir until the gelatine has completely dissolved.

Pour into four 150ml/5fl oz pudding moulds. With a teaspoon drizzle in a little of the fruit juice from the cooked fruits into the desserts and swirl with the handle of a teaspoon for a marbled effect. Chill for 4 hours or until set.

Dip each mould, one at a time, into a bowl of hot water, count to four, then remove from the water, loosen the tops of the panna cotta with a fingertip and turn out onto a serving plate. Stir the remaining fruits and the raspberry jam into the gently cooked fruits, spoon around the panna cotta and serve.

COOK'S TIP Frozen fruits can also be used. Defrost, then use a little of the juice to swirl through the panna cotta, no need to cook half the fruits first.

Autumn

Autumn brings with it a time of change, the greenness of summer now turns to gold and deep orange in a stunning transformation. It is a time of harvest, with a bounty of orchard fruits and vegetable patches generously filled with pumpkins and squashes. Boost energy levels while gardening or out walking with a hearty Sausage Roll or moreish Apple & Cinnamon Oat Bar, then tuck into Mushroom Stew & Dumplings or Butter Chicken with homemade fennel flatbreads when you come in chilly and tired. Spoil friends with a Game Lasagne or roasted Belly Pork with Boulangère Potatoes, followed by Gingered Treacle Tart or Apple Tarte Tatin.

Spinach soup with nutmeg

There are some days when the fridge can look a little bare – a bag of frozen spinach makes a handy standby for this healthy, vibrant-coloured soup that is packed with health-giving antioxidants.

Serves 4
Prep 10 minutes
Cook 20 minutes

25g/1oz butter
200g/7oz onions, chopped
2 garlic cloves, finely chopped
300g/10½oz frozen spinach,
    defrosted
Large pinch freshly grated
    nutmeg
450ml/¾pt vegetable stock
Salt and pepper
2 tbsp Greek-style yogurt

TO FINISH
2 tbsp Greek-style yogurt
Little chopped fresh or
    dried mint

Heat the butter in a saucepan, add the onion and garlic and fry over a low heat for 10 minutes, stirring from time to time until the onions are softened but not browned.

Put the spinach into a sieve and press out the excess water, then add the spinach to the pan with the nutmeg, stock and a little salt and pepper. Bring to the boil then simmer for 5 minutes.

Purée the soup in the saucepan with a stick blender or transfer to a liquidiser, blend then return to the pan. Stir in the yogurt, then taste and adjust the nutmeg and seasoning if needed. Reheat but do not boil, then ladle into bowls and top with spoonfuls of extra yogurt and a sprinkling of mint. Serve with bread and butter.

COOK'S TIP Set the cooker alarm when simmering the soup so that you don't overcook it and lose the bright green colour.

White bean & broccoli soup

*Soup is great for a healthy midweek lunch and can be made a little in advance
— just add the broccoli before serving so that it keeps its bright green colour.*

Serves 4–6
Prep 15 minutes
Cook 27 minutes

1 tbsp vegetable oil
150g/5½oz onion, finely
  chopped
115g/4oz leek, trimmed, finely
  chopped
1 garlic clove, finely chopped
1 stick celery, roughly chopped
1 small bay leaf
2 tbsp fresh chopped parsley
400g/14oz can cannellini
  beans, drained
750ml/26fl oz vegetable stock
Salt and pepper
200g/7oz broccoli, finely
  chopped

TO SERVE
25g/1oz cheddar cheese,
  grated
20ml/4 tsp cold-pressed
  rapeseed oil

Heat the oil in a saucepan then add the onion, leeks, garlic and celery and fry over a medium heat for 5 minutes, stirring from time to time until the vegetables are beginning to soften but not brown.

Add the bay leaf and parsley and fry for 2 minutes. Tip the cannellini beans into a colander, rinse with cold water, drain then add to the pan. Pour in the stock and a little salt and pepper and bring to the boil, then cover and simmer for 15 minutes until the vegetables are cooked through.

Purée the soup in the pan with a stick blender or transfer to a liquidiser and blend to a coarse purée then pour back into the pan. Add the broccoli and stir well, bring to the boil and simmer for 5 minutes until the broccoli is tender. Taste and adjust the seasoning if needed.

Ladle the soup into bowls, top with the cheese and a drizzle of oil. Serve with warm bread and butter.

COOK'S TIP If you prefer chunkier soups, purée half the soup then mix with the rest so that you still have some whole cannellini beans.

Smoked mackerel, potato & beetroot salad

Smoked mackerel is incredible value for money and rich in important omega fatty acids. Here it is given the VIP treatment and served hot on a bed of warm, herby horseradish–dressed potato and beetroot salad with a good portion of watercress for peppery crunch.

Serves 4
Prep 25 minutes
Cook 14–16 minutes

500g/1lb 2oz beetroot, trimmed, peeled, cut into bite-sized pieces
800g/1¾lb potatoes, peeled, cut into bite-sized pieces
100g/3½oz horseradish sauce
15g/½oz fresh dill, chopped
30g/1oz fresh parsley, chopped
salt

DRESSED SQUASH
5 tbsp extra virgin rapeseed oil
200g/7oz butternut squash, peeled, deseeded and cut into small dice
1 lemon, grated zest and juice
2 tbsp chopped fresh dill

TO FINISH
4 hot-smoked mackerel fillets, each about 85g/3oz
70g/2½oz watercress

Half fill the bottom of a steamer with water, bring to the boil, then add the beetroot to the water and the potatoes to the steamer top. Cover and cook for about 10 minutes until tender. Drain the beetroot.

Add the hot vegetables to a bowl with the horseradish sauce, chopped dill and parsley and a little salt, and gently mix together.

For the dressed squash, heat the oil in a large frying pan, add the diced squash and fry over a medium heat, stirring for 2–3 minutes until the squash has softened. Spoon the squash and oil into a bowl and mix with the lemon zest and juice and the remaining dill.

Heat a non-stick frying pan, add the mackerel fillets and cook for 2–3 minutes, turning once until hot through.

Spoon the warm beetroot salad slightly off centre on each of four serving plates and arrange the watercress on top. Peel away the mackerel skin, then arrange a mackerel fillet on top of the watercress on each plate. Spoon over the warm dressed butternut squash and serve immediately.

COOK'S TIP As the butternut squash is pan-fried, make sure to cut it into very small dice so it doesn't take too long to cook.

Squash soup with seed gremolata

The children love to see the different-sized squashes growing in our kitchen gardens at Standen, West Sussex, and Clumber Park, Nottinghamshire, with their bright orange, white or green skins. If using butternut squash or a squash with a thin skin, there is no need to remove this before roasting.

Serves 4–6
Prep 20 minutes
Cook 33 minutes

600g/1lb 5oz squash, weighed after seeds have been scooped out, skin cut away, cut into chunks
1 tbsp vegetable oil
150g/5½oz onion, chopped
½ lemon, grated zest only
115g/4oz carrots, diced
1½ tsp ground ginger
1½ tsp turmeric
1 bay leaf
900ml/1½pt vegetable stock
Salt and pepper

GREMOLATA
1 tbsp pumpkin seeds
10g/¼oz or a large handful of fresh parsley
½ lemon, juice only
2 garlic cloves, chopped
2 tbsp cold-pressed rapeseed oil

Preheat the oven to 160°C/325°F/gas mark 3. Add the squash to a roasting tin and bake in the oven for 40–45 minutes until softened.

Heat the oil in a large saucepan, add the onion and lemon zest and fry over a medium heat for 5 minutes, stirring until softened.

Cut the squash into smaller pieces, add to the onion with the carrots and cook for 2 minutes. Mix in the ground spices and bay leaf and cook for 1 minute. Pour in the stock, season with a little salt and pepper and bring to the boil, stirring. Cover and simmer for 25 minutes.

Purée the soup in the saucepan with a stick blender or transfer to a liquidiser then return to the pan. Adjust with a little extra water or stock and extra seasoning if needed.

To make the gremolata, toast the pumpkin seeds in a dry frying pan for 3–4 minutes until the seeds have just begun to colour and split. Finely chop the parsley, lemon juice and garlic and mix with the oil. Add the seeds and blend briefly until roughly chopped. Spoon into a small bowl.

Reheat the soup, ladle into bowls and spoon over a little gremolata. Serve with bread and butter.

Soya, citrus & chilli beef roll

Brisket gets a makeover, slowly cooked for 3 hours so that it is meltingly soft, then shredded and mixed with soya sauce, chilli, lemon and garlic and served warm in a gluten-free roll with an Asian-inspired salad.

Serves 4
Prep 30 minutes
Cook 3½ hours

565g/1¼lb beef brisket,
   in one piece
1 tbsp vegetable oil
2 tsp sweet smoked paprika
250ml/9fl oz hot water

FOR THE MARINADE
40g/1½oz sweet chilli sauce
6 tbsp soya sauce
½ tsp chilli powder
½ tsp dried chilli flakes
½ lemon, grated zest and
   juice
1 garlic clove, finely chopped

TO FILL
100g/3½oz Romaine lettuce,
   shredded
¼ cucumber, thinly sliced
2 spring onions, finely
   chopped
1 tbsp fresh chopped mint
   leaves
3 tbsp fresh chopped
   coriander leaves
½ lime, grated zest and juice
2 tsp sesame oil
4 large gluten-free rolls
150g/5½oz tomatoes, halved,
   thinly sliced

Preheat the oven to 150°C/300°F/gas mark 2. Trim off any fat from the brisket and, if it is rolled and tied, remove the strings and lay out flat. Brush the surface with the oil then sprinkle over the paprika and rub into the surface of the meat. Put into a small casserole dish with the water. Cover and cook in the oven for 3 hours or until tender.

Remove the brisket from the oven, put on a board, then shred with a knife and fork. Measure the liquid from the dish and make up to 150ml/¼pt with extra water. Return the meat and liquid to the casserole dish.

Mix all the marinade ingredients together and stir into the beef. Return to the oven uncovered and cook for about 30 minutes, stirring a couple of times until the beef is sticky and dark.

For the salad, add the lettuce, cucumber and spring onions to a bowl, add the mint, coriander and lime zest and juice, then add the sesame oil and toss together.

Slit the rolls and open out. Generously spoon the warm beef over the base of the rolls, adding a little of the cooking juices, then spoon over the lettuce salad and sliced tomatoes. Close the rolls and serve. If you would like to take these on a picnic, cook the beef the day before, leave to cool, then refrigerate. Assemble the next day with cold beef and wrap in clingfilm before packing into a plastic container.

COOK'S TIP Check that your sweet chilli sauce and soya sauce are gluten-free if cooking the rolls for anyone with a gluten allergy or intolerance.

Cheese & squash cornbread

Cornbread is hugely popular in America, where it is often served with steaming bowls of chilli, but in the cafés we like to serve these breads warm from the oven on their own or with a bowl of soup. They are gluten-free, too, so great for anyone with an intolerance.

Makes 12 individual breads
Prep 20 minutes
Cook 30–35 minutes

450g/1lb butternut squash, peeled, deseeded, cut into small 1cm/¼ inch dice
500g/1lb 2oz plain gluten-free flour
200g/7oz polenta
1 tsp dried chilli flakes
2 tsp bicarbonate of soda
½ tsp salt
30g/1oz flat-leaf parsley, finely chopped
100g/3½oz cheddar cheese, grated
150g/5½oz smoked cheddar cheese, cubed
2 eggs
345–400ml/12–14fl oz milk
60ml/4 tbsp vegetable oil
25g/1oz pumpkin seeds

Preheat the oven to 180°C/350°F/gas mark 4. Line a 12-hole muffin tray with tulip-shaped paper cases.

Add the butternut squash to a saucepan of boiling water and cook for 5 minutes until just softened, or steam if preferred. Drain well in a colander then tip on to a baking sheet lined with kitchen towel to dry fully.

Add the gluten-free flour, polenta, chilli flakes, bicarbonate of soda and salt to a bowl and stir together, then mix in the chopped parsley and grated cheese.

Add the diced smoked cheese and cooked butternut squash and gently stir into the flour mix.

Beat the eggs, 345ml/12fl oz milk and oil together in a jug. Pour into the flour mix and stir together with a fork until just mixed, adding a little extra milk if needed. Generously fill the muffin cases, sprinkle with the seeds and bake for 25–30 minutes until well risen and golden brown. Remove from the oven, take out of the tin when the muffins are cool enough to handle and leave to cool on a wire rack.

COOK'S TIP The muffin mixture should be the consistency of a loose cake batter, so adjust with a little extra milk or water if you need to. Bakes made with gluten-free flour need more liquid than those made with wheat flour.

The less you mix the muffins the lighter they will be – get them in the oven as quickly as you can after the mix is made for best results.

Pea pesto, mozzarella & spinach panini

We all have a bag of frozen peas in the freezer but here they get a trendy makeover in this tasty nut-free pesto-filled panini.

Serves 4
Prep 20 minutes
Cook 5–8 minutes

300g/10½oz frozen peas
3 tbsp double cream
2 tbsp fresh chopped mint
2 tsp white wine vinegar
2 tsp fresh lemon juice
1 tsp cold-pressed rapeseed oil
1 garlic clove, finely chopped
Salt and pepper
4 panini
2 x 150g/5½oz mozzarella
   balls, drained and thinly
   sliced
3 tomatoes, thinly sliced
50g/1¾oz baby leaf spinach

Put the frozen peas into a bowl, cover with boiling water and leave to stand for 5 minutes until softened, then drain.

Add the peas, cream, mint, vinegar, lemon juice and oil to a food processor. Add the garlic and a little salt and pepper and blend to a coarse purée.

Slice the panini lengthways and open out, then spread the pea pesto on the lower half of each one. Top with the sliced mozzarella and tomatoes, then with the spinach and season lightly. Close the panini and press together.

Preheat your griddle or sandwich toasting machine, then cook the panini until hot and the mozzarella melted. Cut in half and serve with salad.

COOK'S TIP If you don't have a griddle or sandwich toasting machine, preheat a large non-stick frying pan and cook the panini for 3-4 minutes, then carefully turn over, press together and cook the second side until the panini is hot through.

Mushroom, onion & smoked cheddar quiche

This meat-free, gluten-free dish takes the humble quiche to the next level. Generously filled with sage-flavoured mushrooms then topped with lightly caramelised red onion slices and baked with a smoked cheddar custard in a crisp sweet potato crust.

Serves 8
Prep 30 minutes
Cook 61–66 minutes

Little oil for greasing
400g/14oz sweet potato,
    peeled, coarsely grated
1 egg, beaten
50g/1¾oz smoked cheddar,
    grated
¼ tsp dried chilli flakes
Salt and pepper

FILLING
500g/1lb 2oz red onions,
    peeled, topped and tailed
3 tbsp vegetable oil
500g/1lb 2oz mushrooms,
    roughly chopped
2 tbsp fresh chopped sage
100g/3½oz smoked cheddar
    cheese
5 eggs
200ml/7fl oz milk
55ml/2fl oz double cream
3 tbsp fresh chopped parsley
20g/¾oz butter

Preheat the oven to 180°C/350°F/gas mark 4. Lightly brush the base and sides of a loose-bottomed 23cm/9 inch sandwich tin with a little oil. Put the sweet potato into a sieve and squeeze out as much liquid as you can. Add to a bowl and mix in the egg, cheese, chilli and a little salt and pepper and mix well.

Spoon the mixture into the tin and press into an even layer over the base and up the sides with the back of a spoon. Keep a little mixture back and use to patch any holes after baking. Bake for about 15 minutes until the potato is set and beginning to crisp at the edges. Check for any holes and patch with the reserved mixture.

To make the filling, cut the onions into 1cm/½ inch thick circular slices. Add half the oil to a large frying pan, add the onions and fry over a medium heat for about 3 minutes on each side until starting to caramelise. Lift out of the pan and put on a baking sheet.

Add the remaining oil to the frying pan, add the mushrooms and the sage and fry for about 5 minutes until golden and the mushroom juices have evaporated. Spoon the mushroom mix in an even layer into the base of the quiche case, then sprinkle with the grated cheese.

Whisk the eggs, milk and double cream together in a bowl, season with a little salt and pepper then gently pour over the cheese and sprinkle with the parsley. Arrange the onion slices on top of the quiche in circles, using the smaller slices for the centre.

Bake for 30–35 minutes until set. Brush the top with the melted butter and cook for 5 more minutes. Leave to cool slightly then remove from the tin. Serve while still warm, cut into wedges, with buttered new potatoes and a mixed salad.

Turkey koftas & minted yogurt wrap

Koftas are really a cross between a sausage and a meatball. Here low-fat minced turkey is flavoured with parsley, chilli, coriander and lemon, then baked and wrapped in a soft tortilla with a fennel coleslaw and minted yogurt. Serve the koftas straight from the oven, or leave them to cool and pack into a lunchbox for a tasty lunch at your desk or picnic out and about.

Serves 4
Prep 30 minutes
Cook 10–15 minutes

KOFTAS
400g/14oz minced turkey
30g/1oz fresh parsley, chopped
½ tsp dried chilli flakes
2 tsp ground coriander
½ lemon, grated zest and juice
Salt and pepper

COLESLAW
85g/3oz cabbage, coarsely
  grated
85g/3oz carrot, coarsely grated
85g/3oz fennel bulb, coarsely
  grated
2 spring onions, trimmed,
  finely chopped
¼ tsp fennel seeds, roughly
  crushed
½ lemon, grated zest and juice

TO FINISH
115g/4oz Greek-style yogurt
4 tbsp fresh chopped mint
4 large flour tortillas

Preheat the oven to 190°C/375°F/gas mark 5 and line a baking sheet with non-stick baking paper. Add the turkey mince to a large bowl with the parsley, chilli, ground coriander, lemon zest and juice and a little salt and pepper and mix together. Divide into four then shape each into a long sausage around a long metal skewer, so that they are about the same length as the flour tortillas are wide.

Transfer to the lined baking sheet and bake for 10–15 minutes, turning once, until lightly browned and cooked through.

While the koftas bake, make the coleslaw. Add all the ingredients to a bowl and toss together with a little salt and pepper.

For the dressing, mix the yogurt with the mint and a little salt and pepper. Spread all over the flour tortillas. Slide the warm koftas from the skewers, add to the tortillas then cover with the coleslaw. Fold in the ends of the tortillas, then roll up. Cut in half and serve warm with salad or, if preferred, leave the koftas to go cold then assemble and roll the wraps. Wrap in non-stick baking paper or clingfilm, chill for 30 minutes in the fridge for easy slicing, then pack into a lunchbox.

COOK'S TIP If you have a food processor, fit the coarse grater disc and make light work of preparing the vegetables for the slaw.

Choose your favourite type of cabbage for the slaw – white, red or Savoy all work well.

Sausage rolls with apple

Sausage rolls have an enduring appeal – great to add to a packed lunch with a thermos flask or bottle of local cider when out and about at the weekend, or eaten while still warm from the oven when it's too wet to venture outside.

Makes 8
Prep 25 minutes
Cook 25 minutes

115g/4oz red onion, finely
    chopped
4 tbsp fresh chopped parsley
2 tsp fresh chopped thyme
    leaves, plus few extra leaves
    for decoration
40g/1½oz fresh breadcrumbs
115g/4oz Bramley apple,
    peeled, cored, diced
500g/1lb 2oz pork
    sausagemeat
Salt and pepper
1 tbsp water
500g/18oz puff pastry
Little plain flour for dusting
Beaten egg for glazing
Little coarse sea salt, optional

Preheat the oven to 200°C/400°F/gas mark 6.

Add the chopped onion, parsley, thyme, breadcrumbs and apple to a large bowl, then add the sausagemeat, a generous sprinkling of salt and pepper and the water. Mix together well.

Roll the pastry out on a board dusted with a little flour and trim to a rectangle, 45 x 15 cm/18 x 6in. Brush a band of egg down each long side of the pastry, then spoon the sausagemeat in a thick strip down the centre of the pastry.

Roll the pastry over the sausagemeat and brush the pastry with more egg to seal. Roll over so that the join is underneath, then cut into eight sausage rolls. Transfer to the baking sheet, slash the tops with a small knife, then brush with a little more egg. Sprinkle with some coarse salt if liked.

Bake for 25–30 minutes until puffed and golden and the centre is piping hot. Loosen the sausage rolls with a palette knife and transfer to a wire rack to cool.

COOK'S TIP Make sure to press the join of pastry together well and put them underneath the sausage rolls when they cook so that the pastry doesn't burst open.

Windfall apples are perfect for this recipe. If you don't have any Bramley apples, choose a tart dessert apple instead.

Sweet potato curry, chickpea & spinach and chana & beetroot pachadi

Curries needn't be eye-wateringly hot to be good, as this mild mellow curry proves. Packed with a mix of Indian spices and curry paste, the dry spinach and chickpea chana complements the saucy sweet potato and squash curry, while the ruby-red beetroot raita-style pachadi adds a gentle hint of coconut. If you are feeling extra hungry, serve with a spoonful of plain rice too.

Serves 4
Prep 30 minutes
Cook 35 minutes

FOR THE CHANA
1 tbsp vegetable oil
150g/5½oz onions, finely chopped
2 garlic cloves, finely chopped
20g/¾z tikka curry paste
1½ tsp ground coriander
¾ tsp ground cumin
115g/4oz frozen spinach, no need to defrost
salt
400g/14oz can chickpeas, drained, rinsed with cold water and drained again
1 tsp garam masala
½ lemon, grated zest and juice
3 tbsp fresh chopped parsley

For the chana, heat the oil in a saucepan over a high heat, add the onion and garlic and fry for 5 minutes, stirring until lightly coloured and softened.

Add the tikka curry paste, coriander, cumin and spinach and a generous pinch of salt, and continue to cook until the spinach has defrosted and released all its liquid.

Stir in the chickpeas, garam masala, lemon zest and juice and the parsley, stir well and put to one side.

For the curry, heat the oil in a second saucepan, add the onion and tikka curry paste and fry for 3 minutes, stirring. Add the squash and sweet potato, stir well and cook for 2 minutes.

Mix in the tomatoes and tomato purée, then pour in vegetable stock or water to just cover the vegetables. Bring to the boil, then cover and simmer for 15 minutes until the vegetables are just softening.

Pour in the coconut milk. Bring to the boil, stirring, then cook gently, uncovered, for 10 minutes until the vegetables are tender. Taste and adjust the seasoning and add the lemon zest and juice.

FOR THE CURRY

1 tbsp vegetable oil

200g/7oz onions, finely
chopped

40g/1½oz tikka curry paste

170g/6oz butternut squash,
peeled, deseeded, cubed

300g/10½oz sweet potato,
peeled, cubed

170g/6oz tomatoes, roughly
chopped

1 tbsp tomato purée

200ml/7fl oz vegetable stock
or water

½ x 400g/14oz can full fat
coconut milk

½ lemon, grated zest and
juice

BEETROOT PACHADI

40g/1½oz desiccated coconut

1½ tsp ground ginger

½ tsp ground cumin

1 tsp ground coriander

150ml/¼pt water

170g/6oz beetroot, trimmed,
peeled, grated

2 tbsp natural yogurt

For the beetroot pachadi, add the coconut to a small saucepan with the ginger, cumin and coriander, pour in the water until the coconut is just covered, then bring to the boil, stirring to cook the spices. Take off the heat and leave to cool slightly.

Stir the beetroot and yogurt into the coconut mix and spoon into a bowl. Reheat the chana, then spoon into shallow bowls with the hot sweet potato curry and spoonfuls of the pachadi.

COOK'S TIP Try swapping the butternut squash for seasonal pumpkins, try the Crown Prince variety with its golden colour and nutty flavour.

Lamb & Hawkshead Red ale stew

This dish was created by the team who work in the Sticklebarn, a pub in the Lake District owned and run by the Trust. It celebrates the local Herdwick lamb, an ancient but now rare breed of sheep famously farmed by Beatrix Potter, and award-winning Hawkshead Red beer, a local bitter made in an independent brewery with just five brewers. It's the English hops and Dark Crystal malt that give the beer its red colour and bittersweet, rich and fruity flavour which, when slowly cooked with lamb, makes the most delicious meltingly tender stew.

Serves 4
Prep 20 minutes
Cook 3–5 hours

LAMB STEW
1 tbsp vegetable oil
200g/7oz red onions, roughly chopped
2 garlic cloves, finely chopped
1 tsp dark brown sugar
4 tbsp red wine
1 tbsp balsamic vinegar
170ml/6fl oz Hawkshead Red beer
600g/1lb 5oz Herdwick lamb shoulder, diced
2 stems fresh rosemary, leaves picked off the stalks
Salt
1 tbsp tomato purée
1 bay leaf
150–300ml/5–10fl oz lamb or beef stock
1 tbsp cornflour, optional

Heat the oil in a large saucepan, add the red onions and garlic and cook over a medium heat, stirring from time to time, for about 20 minutes until caramelised. Stir in the brown sugar and cook for a further 3–5 minutes until the sugar has become a sticky glaze.

Deglaze the pan with the red wine and balsamic vinegar, adding a little splash of beer. Continue to cook for 3–4 minutes until reduced by half.

Add the diced lamb, rosemary and a little salt and stir so that the meat is coated with the onion and wine reduction. Cover and cook over a low heat for 30–40 minutes, stirring from time to time until the lamb is sealed and has a good colour. Pour in the rest of the beer, the tomato purée and the bay leaf. Cover and simmer gently for 2–4 hours or until the meat is tender, stirring occasionally so that the meat doesn't catch on the bottom of the pan and topping up the liquid with stock as needed.

Meanwhile, preheat the oven to 190°C/375°F/gas mark 5. Add the new potatoes to a roasting tin. Mix 2 tablespoons of the oil with the chopped garlic and drizzle over the potatoes. Sprinkle with the salt and roast in the oven for 20 minutes.

ROASTED VEGETABLES

300g/10½oz small new
   potatoes, scrubbed, halved
3 tbsp vegetable oil
2 garlic cloves, finely chopped
125g/4½oz carrots, halved,
   thinly sliced
140g/5oz celery, thinly sliced
140g/5oz or 8 small pickling
   onions or shallots, peeled,
   halved

Add the carrots, celery and onions to the potatoes, drizzle with the remaining oil and stir together. Bake for 20–30 minutes until tender and lightly browned. Cover and set aside until the lamb is cooked.

Add the roasted vegetables to the lamb stew, cook for 10 minutes until piping hot. Taste and adjust the seasoning with salt and pepper and thicken the sauce with a little cornflour, mixed with a little water if needed.

Ladle into bowls and serve with tumblers of Hawkshead red beer.

COOK'S TIP If you don't live near the Lake District then a large half shoulder of lamb from the supermarket can be used instead. Take the meat off the bone and dice. Alternatively, try using a diced fillet of lamb. Substitute a fruity craft beer or stout in place of the specialist beer above.

Butter chicken curry

Marinating chicken in an easy blend of yogurt, lemon and ready-made curry paste really brings out the flavour and helps to tenderise the chicken. The longer you leave it the more flavour it will have. Prep this the night before and you will feel as if dinner is well on the way when you get home from work next day.

Serves 4
Prep 30 minutes
Marinate 4 hours or overnight
Cook 30 minutes

2 tbsp Greek-style yogurt
½ lemon, grated zest and juice
1 tbsp tikka curry paste
400g/14oz boneless, skinless chicken thighs, cubed
25g/1oz butter
1½ tsp garam masala
½ tsp turmeric
150g/5½oz tomatoes, chopped
1 tbsp tomato purée
1 tsp honey
345ml/12fl oz chicken stock
Salt and pepper
25ml/2 tbsp double cream
25g/1oz celery tops, roughly chopped
2 tbsp fresh chopped coriander

FENNEL FLATBREADS
200g/7oz self-raising flour
1 tbsp Greek-style yogurt
1 tsp fennel seeds, roughly crushed
5–6 tbsp cold water
1 tsp vegetable oil

Mix the yogurt, lemon zest and juice and tikka paste in a large bowl. Add the chicken, stir well to evenly coat in the yogurt mix, then cover the bowl with clingfilm and chill in the fridge for 4 hours, or overnight if you have time.

Melt the butter in a saucepan, add ½ teaspoon of garam masala and the turmeric and fry gently for 1 minute to release the flavour. Add the chicken and the marinade to the pan and cook over a low heat for 10 minutes, stirring from time to time.

Stir in the tomatoes and tomato purée then mix in the honey and enough stock or water to cover the chicken. Season with a little salt and pepper. Bring to the boil, then cover and simmer over a medium heat for 10 minutes, stirring from time to time until the chicken is cooked through.

While the chicken cooks, make the flatbreads. Preheat the oven to 190°C/375°F/gas mark 5. Add the flour, yogurt, fennel seeds and a little salt and pepper to a bowl and gradually stir in enough water to mix to a soft but not sticky dough. Cut into four pieces. Roll out each piece out on a lightly floured surface to a rough oval shape about the size of your hand. Add to a hot, dry frying pan for 1–2 minutes to brown. Brush a baking sheet with the oil and add the breads. Bake for 5 minutes, then turn over and cook for 1 more minute.

Reduce the heat under the curry then stir in the cream and cook for 2 minutes until the sauce is rich and creamy. Stir in the celery tops, the remaining garam masala and chopped coriander and warm through.

Ladle the curry into bowls and serve with the warm breads, torn or cut into pieces.

Mushroom stew & dumplings

Dried mushrooms add a rich, earthy flavour to any casserole or soup. Here they are ground to a powder and mixed with water to make a rich sauce that bathes a mix of fresh mushrooms and chestnuts topped with homely dumplings – the perfect supper dish for when the evenings begin to get colder.

Serves 4
Prep 20 minutes
Cook 55 minutes

30g/1oz dried porcini or
   mixed mushrooms
100ml/3½fl oz boiling water
1 tbsp vegetable oil
300g/10½oz onions, roughly
   chopped
2 garlic cloves, finely chopped
225g/8oz carrots, roughly
   chopped
½ tsp dried marjoram
2 stems fresh thyme, tied with
   string
300g/10½oz mushrooms:
   closed chestnut mushrooms
   or a mix of different types,
   roughly chopped
Salt and pepper
4 tbsp white wine
85g/3oz peeled chestnuts,
   halved
2 tsp cornflour

DUMPLINGS
115g/4oz self-raising flour
55g/2oz vegetarian suet
1 tsp fresh chopped tarragon
   plus extra to garnish
5–6 tbsp cold water

Blitz the dried mushrooms in a food processor or liquidiser until a powder, tip into a bowl then pour over the boiling water and leave to stand while cooking the vegetables.

Heat the oil in a large saucepan, add the onions, garlic and carrots and fry over a medium heat for 15 minutes, stirring from time to time until the onions are soft and lightly coloured.

Add the marjoram and thyme then the mushrooms, increase the heat slightly and fry for around 10 minutes, stirring until the mushrooms are coloured and releasing liquid. Season with salt and pepper. Stir in the white wine to deglaze the pan.

Add the soaked dried mushroom mix with enough extra water to cover the ingredients, about 450ml/16fl oz. Bring to the boil then cover and simmer for 10 minutes or until the carrots are soft. Stir in the chestnuts.

Mix the cornflour with a little water in a small bowl to make a paste, then stir into the mushroom stew and stir until thickened.

To make the dumplings, add the flour, suet, chopped tarragon and a little salt and pepper to a bowl. Stir in enough cold water to make a smooth soft dough. Cut into eight pieces, then roll each piece in your hand to make a ball. Gently drop into the stew, cover the pan and simmer for 10 minutes or until the dumplings have doubled in size and look light and fluffy.

Turn the dumplings with a spoon, recover the pan and cook for a further 10 minutes. Spoon into bowls, discarding the thyme stems, and garnish with a little extra chopped tarragon.

Toasted sweetcorn & cous cous salad

Fed up with sandwiches? Try this quick and easy cous cous salad instead. You can even make it the night before, but don't add the avocado until the last minute so that it stays bright green.

Serves 4
Prep 15 minutes
Cook 10–15 minutes

300ml/½pt vegetable stock
140g/5oz cous cous
2 tbsp cold-pressed rapeseed
  oil
340g/12oz frozen sweetcorn
3 sticks celery, finely chopped
1 red pepper, cored, deseeded,
  finely chopped
15g/½oz fresh coriander,
  chopped
¼–½ tsp dried crushed chilli
  flakes to taste
2 avocados, peeled and stoned
1 lime, grated zest and juice
Salt and pepper
Little extra rapeseed oil to
  serve, optional

Preheat the oven to 180°C/350°C/gas mark 4. Pour the vegetable stock into a saucepan, bring to the boil then take the pan off the heat. Add the cous cous, stir in the oil and leave to cool.

Toast the sweetcorn in a dry frying pan until lightly coloured.

Add the celery, red pepper, coriander and chilli flakes to a large bowl. Fluff up the cous cous with a fork then add to the bowl with the sweetcorn and gently fold together. Set aside until ready to serve.

Chop the avocado, then mix with the lime zest and juice until well coated. Fold into the salad then add salt and pepper to taste. Spoon into bowls to serve and drizzle with a little extra oil if liked.

COOK'S TIP Mix and match other vegetables with the sweetcorn depending on what you have. Perhaps a little diced tomato or a few sliced mushrooms, or some leftover roasted sweet potato or roasted mixed vegetables.

Deep-dish cheese & double potato tart

Packed with autumn vegetables, this rustic pie epitomises the bounty of harvest festival. Serve warm from the oven with roasted vegetables.

Serves 8
Prep 30 minutes
Chill 15 minutes
Cook 42–57 minutes

PASTRY
125g/4½oz wholemeal flour
125g/4½oz plain flour, plus
    extra for dusting
125g/4½oz butter, diced
1 tsp dried mixed herbs
Salt and pepper
1 egg, beaten
2–3 tsp cold water

FILLING
150g/5½oz sweet potato,
    diced
150g/5½oz cauliflower, cut
    into florets
300g/10½oz potatoes, diced
    and cooked
15g/½oz butter
1 tbsp vegetable oil
225g/8oz onions, sliced
2 garlic cloves, finely chopped
50g/1¾oz spinach, roughly
    chopped
10g/¼ oz chopped parsley
¼ tsp grated nutmeg
170g/6oz mature cheddar
    cheese, grated

To make the pastry, add the flour to a bowl or food processor. Add the butter and rub in until fine crumbs, then stir in the mixed herbs and a little salt and pepper. Mix in the egg, then gradually mix in enough water to bring the crumbs together to make a dough. Lightly knead, then roll out on a surface lightly dusted with flour until a little larger than a 23cm/9 inch deep sandwich or tart tin.

Lift the pastry over the rolling pin, lay in the tin and gently press up the sides of the tin. Trim off the excess pastry, prick the base and chill for 15 minutes, or longer if you have time.

Preheat the oven to 180°C/350°F/gas mark 4. Line the tart case with a circle of non-stick baking paper and fill with baking beans. Put the tin on a baking sheet and bake for 10 minutes. Carefully remove the paper and beans and cook for 5 more minutes until the tart is crisp and dry.

Meanwhile, make the filling. Steam the sweet potato and cauliflower over a pan of boiling water for 5–10 minutes until just softening. Add to a bowl with the cold cooked potatoes.

Melt the butter and oil in a frying pan, add the onions and fry over a medium heat for 10 minutes, stirring from time to time until soft and pale golden. Add the garlic and fry for 2 more minutes. Add to the bowl of potato and cauliflower, then add the spinach, parsley, nutmeg and plenty of salt and pepper and mix together.

Mix two thirds of the cheese into the vegetables, then spoon the filling into the tart case. Sprinkle with the rest of the cheese then bake for 30–45 minutes until golden brown.

Leave the pie to cool in the tin for 10 minutes. Loosen the pastry edge then remove from the tin and cut into thick wedges.

Game lasagne

*Ask your butcher for mixed game or, if you have difficulty finding it,
use diced venison and finely chop it in a food processor at home.*

Serves 4
Prep 25 minutes
**Cook 1 hour 12 minutes –
   1 hour 22 minutes**

1 tbsp vegetable oil
175g/6oz onions, finely
   chopped
115g/4oz carrots, diced
2 sticks celery, diced
2 garlic cloves, finely chopped
400g/14oz minced mixed game
100ml/3½fl oz red wine
400g/14oz can chopped
   tomatoes
2 stems fresh rosemary,
   leaves chopped
2 stems fresh thyme, leaves
   chopped
Salt and pepper

CHEESE SAUCE
20g/¾oz butter
20g/¾oz plain flour
250ml/9fl oz milk
85g/3oz cheddar cheese,
   grated
115g/4oz or 6 sheets dried
   lasagne

Heat the oil in a saucepan, add the onion, carrots, celery and garlic and fry over a medium heat for 5 minutes, stirring from time to time until softened. Mix in the minced game and fry for 5 minutes, stirring until evenly browned.

Pour in the red wine, chopped tomatoes and herbs then season with a little salt and pepper and bring to the boil. Simmer for 15 minutes, stirring from time to time until the sauce has thickened slightly.

To make the cheese sauce, melt the butter in a medium saucepan, stir in the flour to make a roux and cook for 2 minutes. Gradually whisk in the milk and cook for 2–3 minutes, still whisking, until smooth and thickened. Stir in two thirds of the cheese and season with salt and pepper.

Spoon a layer of the game mixture into the bottom of an 18cm/7 inch square ovenproof dish, then cover with two sheets of lasagne. Repeat to make three layers of each ending with a layer of pasta. Pour the cheese sauce over the top, sprinkle with the remaining grated cheese and loosely cover with oiled foil. Bake in the oven for 30 minutes. Remove the foil and cook for 15–25 minutes more until the topping is golden brown and bubbling.

Leave to stand for 10 minutes, then cut into four portions and transfer to serving plates. Serve with roasted vegetables or a mixed salad.

COOK'S TIP For roasted vegetables to serve with the lasagne, mix 85g/3oz roughly chopped fennel, 55g/2oz diced carrot, 85g/3oz peeled and deseeded squash, 70g/2½oz sliced leeks with 2 tbsp vegetable oil and salt and pepper in a roasting tin. Roast at 180°C/350°F/gas mark 4 for 30–40 minutes, turning once or twice until lightly browned and tender.

Belly pork, caramelised apple & boulangère potatoes

A weekend roast dinner is the ultimate comfort food, but if you are not a very experienced cook getting everything on the table at the same time can be tricky. With this recipe, the pork and gravy is made the day before and the French-style baked potatoes just do their own thing in the oven, so you just have the apples to finish off at the last minute.

Serves 4
Prep 45 minutes, plus 6 hours to chill
Cook 2½ hours–2 hours 35 minutes

1 tbsp vegetable oil
85g/3oz onion, roughly chopped
85g/3oz carrot, roughly chopped
2 garlic cloves, roughly chopped
4 tbsp white wine
500ml/18fl oz pork or chicken stock
1kg/2¼lb boneless belly pork in one piece, rind scored
3 tsp cornflour

Preheat the oven to 160°C/325°F/gas mark 3. Heat the oil in a frying pan, add the onion, carrots and garlic and fry over a medium heat for 5 minutes. Stir in the wine and deglaze the pan. Pour in 250ml/9fl oz of the stock and bring to the boil, then transfer to a roasting tin. Arrange the piece of pork on top of the vegetables and cover with foil, sealing over the edges of the tin. Transfer to the oven and roast for 2 hours until the pork is very tender.

Leave the pork to sit for 5 minutes, then transfer it to a china dish of similar size or a large loaf tin. Cover with clingfilm then a baking sheet or smaller loaf tin and weight down with cans from the cupboard. When cold, transfer to the fridge and chill for 6 hours or overnight.

Transfer the roasting tin to the hob and mix in the remaining 250ml/9fl oz stock to the now reduced stock and vegetables. Bring to the boil, stirring. Strain through a sieve set over a bowl, pushing through as much of the vegetables as you can. Mix the cornflour with a little water to make a smooth paste, then stir into the gravy with a little salt and pepper. Cover and transfer the gravy to the fridge when cool enough.

BOULANGÈRE POTATOES
15g/½oz butter, melted
600g/1lb 5oz potatoes, peeled,
    thinly sliced
175g/6oz onion, thinly sliced
2 stems fresh rosemary, leaves
    finely chopped
Salt and pepper
300ml/½pt hot chicken or
    vegetable stock

CARAMELISED APPLES
15g/½oz butter
1 tsp caster sugar
2 dessert apples, halved but
    not cored

To serve, preheat the oven to 180°C/350°F/gas mark 4. Grease the base and sides of a 1.2ltr/2pt ovenproof dish with a little of the melted butter. Layer the potatoes, sliced onions and rosemary in the dish, sprinkling the layers with a little salt and pepper. Pour over the hot stock, then brush with the remaining melted butter and sprinkle with a little extra salt and pepper. Bake uncovered for about 1 hour until the potatoes are soft and the top is golden.

Cut the pork into four even-sized pieces, place in a roasting tin and roast above the potatoes for 25–30 minutes or until piping hot and a meat thermometer reads 75°C/165°F and the pork skin is crisp and golden.

Meanwhile, cook the apples by heating the butter and sugar in a small frying pan. Add the apples, cut-side downwards and fry gently until the apples are soft and the cut side is caramelised, turning once.

Pour the gravy into a small saucepan and bring to the boil stirring until thickened and smooth, about 2 minutes. Transfer the pork to serving plates, add spoonfuls of the boulangère potatoes, a baked apple half and some gravy.

COOK'S TIP If you find that the pork skin hasn't crisped up, transfer the roasting tin to a preheated grill and grill for 4–5 minutes or, if you have a cook's blowtorch, use this instead.

Gingered treacle tart

One of those delicious nostalgic puddings that transports you back in time. This deep dish version is flavoured with chopped stem ginger, lemon and orange and is perfect served warm drizzled with custard or topped with a scoop of vanilla ice cream.

Serves 8–10
Prep 35 minutes
Chilling 15 minutes
Cook 35 minutes

PASTRY

125g/4½oz wholemeal flour
125g/4½oz plain flour, plus
   extra for dusting
125g/4½oz butter, diced
40g/1½oz icing sugar
1 egg, beaten
2–3 tsp water

FILLING

375g/13oz golden syrup, plus a
   little extra
50g/1¾oz black treacle
1 egg, beaten
55g/2oz drained stem ginger,
   chopped
300g/10½oz fresh white
   breadcrumbs
½ lemon, skin pared away
   with a vegetable peeler, juice
   squeezed
½ small orange, skin pared
   away with a vegetable
   peeler, juice squeezed

To make the pastry, add the flour to a bowl or food processor. Add the butter and rub in until fine crumbs, then stir in the icing sugar. Mix in the egg, then gradually mix in enough water to bring the crumbs together to a dough. Lightly knead, then roll out on a surface lightly dusted with flour until a little larger than a 23cm/9 inch sandwich tin or deep fluted tart tin.

Lift the pastry over the rolling pin, lay in the tin and gently press up the sides of the tin. Trim off the excess pastry. Prick the base with a fork and chill for 15 minutes, or longer if time.

Preheat the oven to 180°C/350°F/gas mark 4. Line the pastry case with a square of crumpled baking paper then fill with baking beans. Put the tin on a baking sheet and bake for 10 minutes. Carefully remove the paper and beans and cook for 5 more minutes until the pastry case is crisp and dry.

Meanwhile, mix the golden syrup and treacle together in a large bowl. Stir in the egg and ginger, then gradually mix in the breadcrumbs, lemon and orange juice. Spoon into the pastry case and press down with the back of a spoon. Lower the oven temperature to 160°C/325°F/gas mark 3 and bake the tart for 20 minutes or until set.

Cut the pared lemon and orange zest into very thin strips, sprinkle over the tart and drizzle with a little extra syrup, if liked. Leave until almost cool then remove the tin and transfer to a serving plate. Cut into wedges and serve with hot custard or scoops of ice cream.

COOK'S TIP If you have the end of a loaf in the bread bin that isn't quite as fresh as it could be, trim off the crust, cut into cubes and blitz in the food processor to make fine crumbs. Tip into a plastic bag and freeze until needed.

Pumpkin pie

Pumpkins needn't mean just lanterns. This American classic is gently spiced with ground ginger and cinnamon and mixed with cream and light muscovado sugar for a truly autumnal dessert. Try serving with whipped cream flavoured with a little vanilla and dusted with a little cinnamon.

Serves 8–10
Prep 30 minutes
Chill 15 minutes
Cook 1 ½ hours–1 hour 40 minutes

PASTRY
250g/9oz wholemeal flour
60g/2 ¼ oz butter, diced
60g/2 ¼ oz soft margarine
40g/1 ½ oz icing sugar
1 egg, beaten
2–3 tsp cold water

FILLING
1.1kg/2lb 7oz pumpkin, whole weight, washed
2 eggs
120ml/4fl oz double cream
100g/3 ½ oz light muscovado sugar
¾ tsp ground ginger
1 ¼ tsp ground cinnamon

To make the pastry, add the flour, butter, margarine and icing sugar to a bowl and rub in the fat with fingertips or an electric mixer until it resembles fine crumbs. Mix in the egg, then gradually mix in enough water to bring the crumbs together to a dough.

Lightly knead, then roll out on a surface lightly dusted with flour until a little larger than a 23cm/9 inch loose-bottomed sandwich tin or deep fluted tart tin. Lift the pastry into the tin and press over the base and up the sides. Trim off the excess pastry, prick the base with a fork, then chill for 15 minutes or longer if time.

Preheat the oven to 180°C/350°F/gas mark 4. Line the pastry case with a square of crumpled non-stick baking paper then fill with baking beans. Put on a baking sheet and bake for 10 minutes. Carefully remove the paper and beans and cook for 5 more minutes until the base is crisp and dry.

Meanwhile, cut the pumpkin in half, scoop out the seeds and steam for about 40–45 minutes until the flesh is soft. Scoop out the flesh with a spoon, put into a sieve and press out any liquid, then blend in a food processor until smooth.

Add the eggs, cream and sugar to a large bowl, then add the ginger and cinnamon. Whisk until smooth, add the pumpkin purée and whisk until smooth once more.

Pour into the pastry case and bake for about 35–40 minutes until the filling is set but with a slight wobble in the centre. Leave to cool, then cut into wedges and serve with extra cream.

COOK'S TIP If you don't have a steamer you can cover the cut surface of the pumpkin halves with foil, put into a roasting tin and bake at 180°C/350°F/gas mark 4 for about 1–1 ¼ hours until soft.

Apple & cinnamon oat bars

Flapjack-style bars are always popular. This version has a thin ribbon of cooked apple running through the centre, sandwiched between cinnamon-spiced oats.

Makes 14 bars
Prep 25 minutes
Cook 40–45 minutes

450g/1lb dessert apples, peeled, quartered, cored, diced
2 tbsp water
225g/8oz butter or dairy-free margarine
140g/5oz golden syrup
170g/6oz caster sugar
700g/1lb 9oz porridge oats
2 tsp ground cinnamon

Preheat the oven to 180°C/350°F/gas mark 4. Line a 20 x 30 x 4cm/ 8 x 12 x 1½ inch shallow rectangular cake tin with a large piece of non-stick baking paper, snip diagonally into the corners, then press into the tin so that the base and sides are lined with paper.

Add the apples and water to a saucepan, cook over a low heat for 5 minutes, stirring from time until soft. Take off the heat, break up any large pieces of apple with a spoon and leave to cool.

Add the butter or dairy-free margarine to a saucepan with the syrup and sugar and heat over a medium heat, stirring until the fat has melted. Take off the heat.

Add the oats and cinnamon to a large bowl and stir together. Add the melted mixture to the oats and stir well.

Spoon half the oat mixture into the base of the prepared tin and press down firmly with the back of a spoon. Spoon the cooked apple over the top and spread into an even layer. Spoon the remaining oat mixture over the apple and spread roughly so that it just covers the apple.

Bake for about 30–35 minutes or until golden brown on top and firm to the touch. Leave to cool for 15 minutes, mark into 14 bars and leave to cool completely in the tin.

Cut into bars, peel off the paper and remove from the tin to serve.

COOK'S TIP If you only have cooking apples, sweeten with a little sugar when stewing them.

Some people who must avoid gluten can tolerate oats – just make sure that the pack carries the gluten-free symbol as not all oats are packaged in factories that are gluten-free.

Apple tarte tatin

This quite ordinary mix of ingredients produces a wonderful alchemy when baked together. The secret is to melt the butter and dissolve the sugar without stirring, just tilt and swirl the pan to mix to make a rich caramel-like toffee, then add the apples and top with puff pastry for this topsy-turvy tart.

Serves 8
Prep 25 minutes
Cook 20–25 minutes

150g/5½oz caster sugar
70g/2½oz butter, cut into
    4 pieces
6 dessert apples, peeled,
    quarted and cored
250g/9oz puff pastry,
    defrosted if frozen
Little flour for dusting

Preheat the oven to 190°C/375°F/Gas mark 5.

Add the sugar and butter to the base of a 20cm/8 inch frying pan with a metal handle and cook over a high heat without stirring until the butter has melted and the sugar dissolved. Swirl the pan gently to encourage any stubborn sugar grains to dissolve and for the syrup to colour evenly. Continue cooking until the sugar becomes a golden caramel, this will take about 5 minutes from when you begin heating the pan.

Quickly take the pan off the heat and add the apples, cored sides uppermost, in two rings. Cool slightly.

Roll the pastry out on a lightly floured surface until a little larger than the frying pan, trimming to a neat circle with a large dinner plate. Lay the pastry over the apples and tuck the edges of the pastry down the sides of the pan around the apples. Make two small holes with a knife for the steam to escape.

Bake in the oven for 20–25 minutes until the pastry is risen and golden brown. Leave to stand for 5 minutes, then cover the top of the pan with a large plate, holding the pan handle with a cloth and the plate firmly, turn upside down so that the apple side is uppermost on the plate. Remove the pan and cut into wedges. Serve with spoonfuls of softly whipped cream.

COOK'S TIP If you don't have a frying pan with an ovenproof handle, pour the hot caramel into a 23cm/9 inch cake tin with a fixed base, add the apples then the pastry and cook as above.

Chocolate hazelnut torte fudge cake

Super rich and super dark with just a hint of sweetness, this is a very grown-up chocolate cake with a soft, moist fudgy texture and a hint of toasted hazelnuts.

Serves 10–12
Prep 30 minutes
Cook 40–45 minutes

170g/6oz dark chocolate, broken into pieces
200g/7oz butter or soft margarine
2 tsp vanilla extract
100g/3½oz hazelnuts, toasted, very finely chopped in a food processor
50g/1¾oz cocoa
1 tsp baking powder
5 eggs
150g/5½oz caster sugar
1 tsp salt

FOR THE TOPPING
100ml/3½fl oz double cream
100g/3½oz dark chocolate, broken into pieces
20g/¾oz white chocolate, broken into pieces

Preheat the oven to 150°C/300°F/gas mark 2. Grease and base line a 23cm/9 inch springform tin or deep loose-bottomed sandwich tin with non-stick baking paper.

Melt the chocolate and soft margarine in a saucepan over a low heat, stirring from time to time until smooth. Stir in the vanilla. Leave to cool.

Mix the hazelnuts, cocoa and baking powder in a bowl and set aside.

Add the eggs and sugar to a bowl and whisk with an electric mixer over a low speed, sprinkling in the salt. Increase the speed and whisk for about 5 minutes until the mixture is very thick and will leave a ribbon-like trail when the whisk is lifted out of the bowl and a little of the mixture drizzled over the surface.

Slowly pour the cooled chocolate mixture into the bowl and fold in with a large metal spoon until incorporated. Sprinkle the hazelnut mixture over the top and gently fold together.

Pour into the cake tin, tap once on the work surface, then bake in oven for 45–55 minutes until well risen and a skewer inserted into the centre comes out cleanly. Leave to cool in the tin.

Continued overleaf

Take the torte out of the tin, peel off the lining paper and set on a wire rack over a plate. Pour the cream into a small saucepan, bring to the boil, then take off the heat and add the chocolate. Stir gently until melted and smooth.

Pour the topping over the torte and ease over the top and sides with a palette knife, catching any drips on the plate.

Melt the white chocolate in a bowl set over a saucepan of gently simmering water, then pipe or drizzle from a spoon over the top of the torte in random squiggly lines. Leave to set then transfer the torte to a serving plate and cut into slices to serve.

COOK'S TIP Make sure that the melted chocolate mixture is cool before adding to the eggs.

To toast the hazelnuts, add them to a non-stick frying pan and cook over a medium heat for a few minutes, shaking the pan until the nuts are an even golden brown. Alternatively, put the hazelnuts on a piece of foil set in the base of a grill pan and toast under the grill for a few minutes.

Butter & walnut layer cake

A wonderfully old-fashioned rich buttery sponge, flecked with toasted walnuts, then layered with a honey and vanilla buttercream and topped with crunchy walnut praline for a touch of luxury.

Cuts into 10–12 slices
Prep 30 minutes
Chill 15 minutes
Cook 21–23minutes

200g/7oz butter, at room
    temperature
200g/7oz caster sugar
4 eggs
200g/7oz self-raising flour
1 tsp baking powder
40g/1½oz walnut pieces,
    toasted, chopped

BUTTERCREAM
100g/3½oz butter at room
    temperature or soft
    margarine
50g/1¾oz runny honey
50g/1¾oz icing sugar, sifted
2 tsp vanilla extract

WALNUT PRALINE
70g/2½oz caster sugar
1 tbsp water
40g/1½oz walnut pieces

Preheat the oven to 180°C/350°F/gas mark 4. Grease and base line three 20cm/8 inch sandwich tins with circles of non-stick baking paper.

Cream the butter and sugar together in a bowl with an electric mixer until light and fluffy. Add the eggs, one at a time, beating well after each addition and spooning in a little of the flour to stop the mix from separating.

Gradually mix in the remaining flour and the baking powder until smooth, then fold in the toasted walnuts.

Divide the cake mixture evenly between the three tins and spread level. Bake for 18–20 minutes until well risen, golden brown and the centre springs back when lightly pressed with a fingertip.

Leave to cool in the tins for 5 minutes, then loosen the edge of the cakes with a knife and turn out onto two wire racks. Peel off the lining paper and leave to cool completely.

To make the buttercream, add the butter or soft margarine to a bowl with the honey and beat until smooth with an electric mixer, then beat in the icing sugar and vanilla until light and fluffy.

To make the praline, add the sugar and water to a medium-sized frying pan, and cook over a medium heat without stirring until the sugar has dissolved and become a clear liquid. Tilt the pan to mix if needed. Continue to cook for about 3 minutes until the syrup has turned a rich golden colour. Take the pan off the heat, add the walnuts and stir together. Spoon onto a baking sheet lined with non-stick baking paper and leave to cool and harden.

Transfer one of the cakes to a serving plate, spread the top with one third of the buttercream, then cover with a second cake and repeat. Spread the remaining buttercream over the top of the third cake. Crush the praline by folding the paper over the nuts and bashing with a rolling pin. Sprinkle over the top of the cake and cut into slices to serve.

COOK'S TIP Dissolving the sugar for the praline can be tricky. Resist the urge to stir it, just tilt the pan to mix. Keep your eye on it the whole time, once the edges of the syrup begin to change colour the rest quickly follows, so tilt the pan so that it cooks evenly and take off the heat as soon as it is a golden colour; too dark and the syrup will taste bitter.

To toast the walnuts for the cake, cook the walnuts in a dry frying pan for a few minutes or under the grill until the nuts are just beginning to colour.

Winter

Winter is a time to wrap up warm in woolly scarves and hats; to stride out and marvel at the frosty lawns, white-veiled hedges, feathery grasses and near-naked trees softly lit with low winter sun, before heading home for a steaming bowl of creamy Cauliflower & Stilton soup or jewel-coloured Beetroot & Horseradish soup, or a warming Chicken & Mustard Casserole. For something sweet, try our delicious Sticky Gingerbread, or our special dairy-free Banoffee Cake made with bananas and apples and finished with a coconut frosting.

Beetroot & horseradish soup

Fresh horseradish is a rather neglected vegetable and adds a hot peppery taste to this amazingly coloured soup.

Serves 4–6
Prep 20 minutes
Cook 55 minutes

1 tbsp vegetable oil
150g/5½oz onion, chopped
150g/5½oz, or 1 fennel bulb, roughly chopped
2 sticks celery, roughly chopped
2 garlic cloves, finely chopped
500g/1lb fresh beetroot, trimmed, peeled, diced
900ml/1½pt vegetable stock
1 tsp white wine vinegar
20g/¾oz fresh horseradish, peeled, grated
Salt and pepper
100ml/3½oz double cream, optional
Few snipped chives, optional

Heat the oil in a large saucepan, add the onion and fry over a medium heat for 5 minutes, stirring from time to time. Stir in the fennel, celery and garlic, cover with a lid and cook gently for a further 10 minutes.

Remove the lid from the pan and add the beetroot and stock. Bring to the boil, then cover and simmer for about 40 minutes until the beetroot is soft.

Purée in the pan with a stick blender or transfer to a liquidiser. Add the white vinegar, horseradish and salt and pepper and purée again. Adjust the consistency with a little extra stock if needed. Pour back into pan if in a liquidiser.

Reheat the soup, then ladle into bowls, drizzle with a little cream and a sprinkling of fresh chives, if liked.

COOK'S TIP If fresh horseradish is unavailable, stir in a teaspoonful or two of hot horseradish sauce to taste.

Don't be tempted to use vacuum packs of ready-cooked beetroot; it just doesn't have the same depth of flavour.

Fragrant leek & sweet potato soup

Unusually topped with a zesty lime and smoked mackerel mix, this soup will get your friends talking!

Serves 4–6
Prep 20 minutes
Cook 29–35 minutes

1 tbsp vegetable oil
300g/10½oz leeks, trimmed,
   thinly sliced
300g/10½oz sweet potatoes,
   peeled, diced
1 tbsp finely chopped parsley
   stalks
1 tsp ground coriander
Large pinch to ¼tsp dried
   chilli flakes, to taste
1 cardamom pod, roughly
   crushed
750ml/1¼pt vegetable stock
Salt and pepper

SMOKED MACKEREL TOPPING
1 smoked mackerel fillet about
   85g/3oz, skin removed
2 tbsp mayonnaise
½ lime, grated zest and juice
4 tsp freshly chopped parsley

Heat the oil in a medium saucepan. Reserve the brightest green leek slices or about one quarter of the leeks and add the rest to the pan with the sweet potato. Fry over a medium heat for 5 minutes, stirring from time to time until just beginning to soften.

Stir in the chopped parsley stalks, ground coriander, chilli flakes and cardamom pod and cook for 1 minute. Pour in the stock, season with a little salt and pepper and bring to the boil. Cover and simmer for 20–25 minutes until the vegetables are soft.

Purée the soup in the pan with a stick blender or transfer to a liquidiser then pour back into the pan. Taste and adjust the seasoning if needed, then mix in the reserved sliced leeks and cook for 3–4 minutes, until softened but still bright green.

Meanwhile, break up the mackerel, checking for any bones, and mash with a fork in a small bowl. Stir in the mayonnaise, lime zest and juice, parsley and a little salt and pepper.

Ladle the hot soup into bowls, top with spoonfuls of the mackerel topping and serve with warm bread.

Celeriac & truffle soup

Truffle oil adds an exotic extra to this smooth celeriac soup. If you haven't used it before, look out for it alongside the other oils in the supermarket.

Serves 4–6
Prep 20 minutes
Cook 35 minutes

1 tbsp vegetable oil
200g/7oz onions, roughly
   chopped
½ tsp fennel seeds, roughly
   crushed
1 stick celery, roughly chopped
150g/5½oz potatoes, peeled,
   diced
400g/14oz celeriac, peeled,
   diced
700ml/1¼pt vegetable stock
Salt and pepper
3 tsp truffle oil

Heat the oil in a saucepan, add the onion, fennel seeds and celery and fry over a medium heat for 10 minutes, stirring from time until the onions have softened but not coloured.

Add the potatoes and celeriac and stir well. Pour in the stock, season with salt and pepper and bring to the boil. Cover and simmer for 25 minutes until the vegetables are soft.

Purée with a stick blender in the pan or transfer to a liquidiser and blend until smooth. Stir in half the truffle oil and leave to stand for 5 minutes.

Taste and adjust the seasoning if needed. Reheat and ladle into bowls. Drizzle over the remaining truffle oil and serve with warm bread and butter.

COOK'S TIP This soup also goes well with blue cheese. Omit the truffle oil, ladle the hot soup into bowls, then drizzle over a little double cream and top with a little crumbled St Agur or dolcelatte cheese.

Cauliflower & stilton soup with pickled pear

This soup can be made earlier in the day and just reheated when you are ready to serve. The sliced pickled pears can be packed into glass or plastic containers and kept in the fridge for up to 7 days. The pears also taste delicious served with cold ham or cheese.

Serves 4–6
Prep 20 minutes
Cook 24–30 minutes

1 tbsp vegetable oil
1 onion, about 140g/5oz,
   finely chopped
2 sticks celery, trimmed, diced
2 garlic cloves, finely chopped
1 large cauliflower, trimmed,
   core discarded to give about
   450g/1lb florets
450ml/¾ pt vegetable or
   chicken stock
150ml/¼ pt double cream
Salt and pepper
85g/3oz stilton, rind removed,
   cheese crumbled

PICKLED PEARS
3 tbsp white wine vinegar
3 tbsp water
2 tsp runny or set honey
1 bay leaf
Pinch grated nutmeg
Pinch ground ginger
1 small star anise
1 pear, peeled, quartered,
   cored, sliced

To make the soup, heat the oil in a medium-sized saucepan then add the onion, celery and garlic and fry over a medium heat for 5 minutes, stirring until softened but not coloured.

Add the cauliflower florets to the saucepan and sauté for 5 minutes, stirring until just beginning to soften. Pour in the stock and cream, add a little salt and pepper and bring just to the boil. Reduce heat, cover and simmer gently for 10–15 minutes until the cauliflower is soft.

Add half the stilton to the soup, then purée in the pan with a stick blender or transfer to a liquidiser and blend until smooth, then pour back into the pan. Taste and adjust the seasoning if needed. Leave to cool, then transfer to the fridge until needed.

To make the pickled pears, add the vinegar, water, honey, bay leaf and spices to a small saucepan. Bring to the boil, add the pear slices, then simmer gently for 4–5 minutes until just soft. Remove from the heat, add a little salt and pepper, then cool.

Pack the pears into a glass jar or plastic container, pour over the vinegar mixture, then cover and chill in the fridge for at least 2 hours for the flavours to mingle.

When ready to serve, reheat the soup, ladle into bowls and top with a few slices of drained pickled pear, the remaining crumbled stilton and a little black pepper. Serve with warm bread.

Turkey in bbq sauce

Super tasty and really easy to prepare, serve in bowls with cornbread, chunky pieces of bread or warm garlic bread.

Serves 4
Prep 20 minutes
Cook 35 minutes

400g/14oz minced turkey
Salt and pepper
1 tbsp vegetable oil
150g/5½oz red onion, chopped
150g/5½oz carrots, diced
2 garlic cloves, finely chopped
200g/7oz frozen sweetcorn
1 tsp sweet smoked paprika
500g/1lb 2oz tomatoes, chopped
1 tbsp tomato purée
3 tbsp brown sauce
2 tbsp white wine vinegar
55g/2oz light brown sugar
250ml/9fl oz vegetable stock
2 tbsp fresh chopped parsley
2 tbsp fresh chopped chives to garnish, optional

Preheat the oven to 180°C/350°F/gas mark 4. Add the turkey mince to a small roasting tin, break into small pieces, season with salt and pepper and bake in the oven for 15 minutes.

Meanwhile, heat the oil in a saucepan, add the onion, carrot and garlic and fry over a medium heat for 5 minutes, stirring from time until softened. Stir in the sweetcorn and smoked paprika, chopped tomatoes and tomato purée and bring to the boil.

Stir in the brown sauce, vinegar and sugar, then add just enough stock to cover the vegetables. Bring to the boil. Break up the turkey into pieces with a fork, stir into the sauce, cover and simmer for 20 minutes.

Taste and adjust the seasoning if needed. Stir in the chopped parsley, spoon into bowls and top with the chopped chives, if using. Serve with Cheese and Squash Cornbread (see page 109) or garlic bread.

COOK'S TIP Why not make up a double quantity, eat half for supper, and cool the rest and freeze in a plastic container for another time.

Smoked cheese & spinach frittata

Smoked cheddar adds an unusual and delicious flavour to this
Italian-style spinach, spring onion and potato omelette.

Serves 6
Prep 15 minutes
Cook 23–27 minutes

400g/14oz potatoes, scrubbed,
    cut into 1cm/½inch cubes
100g/3½oz spinach
½ bunch spring onions, thinly
    sliced
6 eggs, beaten
150g/5½oz smoked cheddar
    cheese, grated
1 tsp fresh thyme leaves
Salt and pepper
4 tsp vegetable oil

Preheat the oven to 180°C/350°F/gas mark 4. Add the potatoes to a saucepan of boiling water and cook for 5 minutes until just tender with a slight bite left in the middle. Drain and transfer to a large bowl.

Add the spinach to the drained potato pan with 1 teaspoon of water and cook over a medium heat for 1–2 minutes, stirring until just wilted. Drain the spinach well on kitchen towel, then roughly chop.

Add the spinach to the potatoes with the spring onions and beaten eggs and mix together with a large spoon. Stir in the cheese and thyme, then season with salt and pepper.

Heat the oil in a 23cm/9 inch frying pan with a metal handle, pour in the omelette mix, reduce the heat and cook for about 10 minutes until the bottom is set and golden.

Transfer the pan to the oven and cook for 7–10 minutes until the egg is set and the top is golden. Loosen the omelette edges with a knife then cover the pan with a large plate, holding the pan with a teacloth, turn it upside down, jerk to release the omelette then remove the pan. Cut into wedges and serve warm or cold.

COOK'S TIP If you don't have a frying pan that can go in the oven, finish the omelette off under the grill making sure that the handle is well away from the heat.

Squash, balsamic onion & walnut bruschetta

'Something on toast' is so often a fallback for lunch, and this version lifts it to another level. A deliciously easy squash hummus topped with slowly cooked balsamic onions, crunchy walnuts and peppery watercress is a popular addition to our winter café menu.

Serves 4
Prep 25 minutes
Cook 30 minutes

500g/1lb 2oz butternut squash, peeled, sliced, deseeded, cut into 2cm/¾ inch cubes
4 garlic cloves, left unpeeled
2 tbsp vegetable oil
½ lemon, juice only
1 tbsp crunchy or smooth peanut butter
¼ tsp ground cinnamon
¼ tsp ground cumin
¼ tsp sweet smoked paprika
Salt and pepper

BALSAMIC ONIONS
1 tbsp vegetable oil
350g/12oz red onions, thinly sliced
25g/1oz caster sugar
2 tbsp balsamic vinegar

TO FINISH
4 slices bread cut from a large bloomer or sourdough loaf
40g/1½ oz walnut pieces, lightly toasted
25g/1oz watercress

Preheat the oven to 180°C/350°F/gas mark 4. Scatter the diced squash and unpeeled garlic in a roasting tin, drizzle with 2 tablespoons oil and roast for 30 minutes until softened and just beginning to colour.

To make the balsamic onions, heat the oil in a frying pan, add the onions and fry over a medium heat, for 15 minutes, stirring until very soft. Stir in the sugar and half the vinegar and cook for a few minutes, stirring frequently until the sugar has slightly caramelised and the liquid absorbed. Stir in the remaining vinegar and leave to cool.

Transfer the squash to a food processor. Peel the garlic, add to the processor with the lemon juice, peanut butter, cinnamon, cumin and smoked paprika. Season with a little salt and pepper then blend until smooth. Set aside.

Lightly toast both sides of the bread, spread the squash hummus on top, then add a spoonful of onions and a scattering of toasted walnuts and watercress. Serve with a side salad if liked.

COOK'S TIP For a party or as informal starter, slice and toast a ciabatta bread rather than using a bloomer loaf, then spread over the squash mixture and top with the balsamic onions and watercress.

Turkey enchiladas

Break away from the usual spag bol or chilli and, rather than buying minced beef, opt for low-fat minced turkey instead.

Serves 4
Prep 30 minutes
Cook 50–55 minutes

1 tbsp vegetable oil
115g/4oz red onion, thinly
   sliced
1 tsp ground cumin
1 tsp sweet smoked paprika
½ tsp dried chilli flakes
1 garlic cloves, finely chopped
500g/1lb 2oz minced turkey
400g/14oz can red kidney
   beans
½ red pepper, cored, deseeded,
   thinly sliced
½ orange or yellow pepper,
   cored, deseeded, thinly sliced
115g/4oz tomatoes, chopped
4 tsp tomato purée
1 tbsp each of fresh chopped
   parsley, coriander and mint
Salt and pepper

TO FINISH
4 large tortilla wraps
3 tbsp cold pressed rapeseed oil
150g/5½ oz cheddar cheese,
   grated

TO SERVE
½ cucumber, roughly chopped
115g/4oz cherry tomatoes,
   quartered

Heat the oil in a saucepan, add the onion, spices, chilli flakes and garlic and fry over a medium heat for 5 minutes, stirring until softened. Add the turkey mince, increase the heat and fry for 5 minutes, stirring and breaking up the turkey until coloured.

Rinse and drain the kidney beans. Add the kidney beans and peppers to the pan, then mix in the tomatoes and tomato purée. Reduce the heat, cover and cook for 15 minutes until the turkey is cooked through and the peppers are soft. Add the chopped herbs and adjust the seasoning. Remove from the heat and drain off 150ml/¼ pt of the sauce and set aside.

Separate the wraps then brush with the oil. Spoon the mince mixture in a line down the centre of each wrap. Fold in the ends then roll up and put join-side down in a shallow ovenproof dish. Spoon the strained sauce over the wraps, sprinkle with the cheese, then bake in the oven for 25–30 minutes until piping hot and the cheese is melted and bubbling.

Transfer to serving plates and serve with cucumber, tomatoes and chimchirri sauce, see below.

COOK'S TIP To make the chimchirri sauce, add 40g/1½oz fresh parsley, 40g/1½oz fresh coriander, 2 garlic cloves, 50g/1¾oz red onion, ½ tsp dried chilli flakes, 2 tbsp cold-pressed rapeseed oil, 5 tsp lemon juice, 4 tsp red wine vinegar and a little salt and pepper to a food processor and blend until finely chopped.

Chickpea burger with peanut sauce, slaw and flatbread

Vegetarian burgers can sometimes be a little dull, however this moist, full-flavoured version is anything but. Served with a satay-style creamy sauce and a fresh-tasting slaw salad, it's sure to win over the sceptics.

Serves 4
Prep 35 minutes
Chill 30 minutes
Cook 14 minutes

400g/14oz red onion
2 x 400g/14oz cans chickpeas
½ tsp dried chilli flakes
1 tsp ground cumin
1½ tsp ground coriander
¼ tsp turmeric
2 tbsp fresh chopped parsley
60g/2¼oz gluten-free self-
    raising flour
3 tbsp vegetable oil

SAUCE
1 tsp caster sugar
2 tsp soya sauce
¼ tsp dried chilli flakes
50g/1¾oz peanut butter
70ml/2½fl oz coconut milk
½ lime, juice only

SLAW
170g/6oz red cabbage, thinly
    shredded
125g/4½oz trimmed beetroot,
    peeled, grated
100g/3½oz red onion, thinly
    sliced
½ lime, grated zest and juice

First make the burgers, preheat the oven to 180°C/350°F/gas mark 4. Cut the red onion into chunks, then finely chop in a food processor. Drain and rinse the chickpeas and drain again. Add the chickpeas, chilli flakes, ground spices, parsley and a pinch of salt. Pulse together until the chickpeas are broken down and everything is blended together.

Divide into four mounds on a chopping board, then squeeze each quarter into a ball, roll in the flour and flatten into a burger shape. Chill for 30 minutes to firm up.

Heat the oil in a large frying pan, add the burgers and fry over a medium heat for 2 minutes on each side until golden on both sides. Carefully lift out of the pan and transfer to a baking sheet. Bake in the oven for 10 minutes until piping hot.

Meanwhile, add the sugar, soy sauce, and chilli to a small saucepan bring to the boil over a low heat, then add the peanut butter and coconut milk. Stir until smooth, then take off the heat and mix in the lime sauce.

For the slaw, mix all the ingredients together. Spoon onto serving plates, add the hot burgers, a spoonful of the hot sauce, some chunky pieces of cucumber and warm flatbreads, torn into pieces.

COOK'S TIP The burgers are much more fragile than homemade beef burgers, so turn them carefully in the frying pan with a wide slotted fish slice. If they do break up a little, simply pat back into shape.

Potato, red cabbage & garlic salad

Oven-roasted garlic, peeled and mashed, adds a mellow sweet garlicky flavour to the mayonnaise dressing for a potato salad with a difference. Serve as a light meal or accompany with some cold slices of home-cooked ham or roast turkey for a supper dish.

Serves 4
Prep 20 minutes
Cook 55 minutes

1 bulb garlic
3 tbsp vegetable oil
500g/1lb 2oz potatoes, peeled,
    cut into 2cm/¾ inch cubes
450g/1lb sweet potatoes,
    peeled, cut into 2cm/¾ inch
    cubes
85g/3oz mayonnaise
Salt and pepper
40g/1½ oz blanched almonds,
    toasted, sliced
55g/2oz sultanas
200g/7oz red cabbage, very
    finely shredded
2 tbsp fresh chopped parsley
40g/1½ oz mixed salad leaves,
    torn into bite-sized pieces

Preheat the oven to 180°C/350°F/gas mark 4. Put the whole garlic bulb on a small piece of foil, drizzle with ½ tablespoon of the oil, then wrap the foil around the garlic to enclose completely. Put onto a baking sheet and roast for 45 minutes until soft.

Meanwhile, add the white potatoes to a saucepan of boiling water and cook for 8–10 minutes until partly cooked. Drain. Heat the remaining oil in a roasting tin in the oven for 5 minutes. Add the partly cooked potatoes and the sweet potatoes and toss in the hot oil. Roast for about 40 minutes, turning once or twice until lightly coloured.

Take the garlic out of the oven and leave to cool for 15 minutes. Unwrap the garlic, cut the top off the bulb then squeeze the soft garlic centres out of the papery casing into a bowl, mash with a fork if needed. Mix in the mayonnaise and a little salt and pepper, then add the potatoes, almonds, sultanas, red cabbage and parsley. Add the salad leaves and gently mix together, then spoon into serving dishes.

COOK'S TIP If you have a food processor, attach the fine slicing disc and make quick work of slicing the red cabbage.

Moroccan-style cauliflower salad

There is so much more to cauliflower than just cauliflower cheese, as this spicy salad proves. Sprinkled with jewel-like pomegranate seeds, it is an impressive-looking salad to serve to friends and family.

Serves 4
Prep 20 minutes
Cook 20 minutes

½ cauliflower, inner leaves
    left on
6 tsp vegetable oil
1½ tsp peri peri seasoning
½ tsp turmeric
100g/3½oz leeks, slit
    lengthways, rinsed, thinly
    sliced
400g/14oz can chickpeas,
    drained, rinsed with cold
    water, drained again
15g/½oz flat-leaf parsley,
    roughly chopped
½ pomegranate, seeds only
2 tbsp extra virgin cold-
    pressed rapeseed oil
Salt and pepper
40g/1½oz rocket leaves
Lemon wedges, optional

Preheat the oven to 190°C/375°F/gas mark 5. Put the cauliflower cut-side down on a baking tray and pull back the leaves slightly. Rub the florets and leaves with 4 teaspoons of the vegetable oil. Sprinkle with the peri peri seasoning and turmeric and bake for about 15 minutes until the leaves are blackened and the florets are softened. Remove from the oven and leave to cool for a few minutes.

Trim off the base of the cauliflower stalk then chop the leaves and stem and cut the florets into small pieces.

Heat the remaining vegetable oil in a frying pan, add the leeks and fry over a medium heat for about 5 minutes until they are lightly coloured with a few bits of charring.

Add the cauliflower and leeks to a large bowl, add the chickpeas and parsley and mix together.

Sprinkle over the pomegranate seeds and rapeseed oil, season with a little salt and pepper and mix again.

Divide the rocket between serving bowls then top with the cauliflower salad. Serve with lemon wedges to squeeze over, if liked.

COOK'S TIP To remove the seeds from the pomegranate, hold it cut-side downwards in your hand and bash the top with a rolling pin to release the seeds.

Peri peri seasoning, sometimes written 'piri piri', is a dry Portuguese spice mix made up of chilli, garlic and citrus peel and is sold in jars alongside the other spices in the supermarket.

Chicken & wholegrain mustard casserole

Homely, comforting and just the kind of supper to enjoy curled up on the sofa with a good film.

Serves 4
Prep 20 minutes
Cook 55–60 minutes

2 tbsp vegetable oil
200g/7oz onions, chopped
500g/1lb 2oz boneless skinless
    chicken thighs, diced
200g/7oz parsnips, cut into
    chunks
250g/9oz carrots, cut into
    chunks
250g/9oz potatoes, scrubbed,
    cut into chunks
600ml/1pt hot chicken stock
3 tsp wholegrain mustard
2 tsp honey
3 stems fresh thyme
2 tbsp fresh chopped parsley
Salt and pepper
85g/3oz green cabbage, finely
    shredded, blanched for
    2 minutes in boiling water

Preheat the oven to 180°C/350°F/gas mark 4. Heat the oil in a large frying pan, add the onions and cook over a medium heat for 10–15 minutes, stirring from time to time until lightly coloured.

Add the diced chicken, increase the heat slightly and fry, stirring until the chicken is sealed. Transfer to a casserole dish. Add the parsnips, carrots and potatoes to the casserole dish. Mix the hot stock with the mustard and honey, then pour over the chicken and vegetables to just cover. Add the thyme, parsley and a little salt and pepper.

Cover with a lid and transfer to the oven. Cook for about 45 minutes until the vegetables are soft and the chicken cooked through. Discard the thyme, add the blanched cabbage and stir well. Taste and adjust the seasoning if needed. Ladle into bowls and serve with bread and butter.

COOK'S TIP Don't try to rush frying the onions, this early stage will add plenty of flavour and added sweetness to the finished dish.

Smoked mackerel fishcake, celeriac remoulade & pickled vegetables

Nutritionists recommend that we all try to eat more oily fish. Smoked mackerel is rich in health-boosting omega 3 and 6 fats and is ready to use straight from the pack. It's delicious mixed with fresh horseradish and parsley for these super-sized fishcakes, which are accompanied by a celeriac twist on coleslaw and this colourful, easy-to-make pickle.

Serves 4
Prep 30 minutes
Cook 29–39 minutes

FISHCAKES

600g/1lb 5oz potatoes, peeled, diced
340g/12oz smoked mackerel fillets, skinned
25g/1oz fresh horseradish, peeled, grated or 2 tsp hot horseradish sauce from a jar
1 tbsp mayonnaise
1 egg, beaten
Salt and pepper
15g/½oz fresh parsley, chopped
100g/3½oz fresh breadcrumbs
2–3 tbsp vegetable oil

CELERIAC REMOULADE

225g/8oz celeriac, peeled
2 tsp wholegrain mustard
3 tbsp mayonnaise
½ lemon, juice only

Add the potatoes to a saucepan of boiling water and cook for 15–20 minutes or until soft. Drain then mash lightly, leaving some chunks, then set aside to cool.

Check the mackerel for any bones, then shred the fish into flakes with two forks.

Add the horseradish, mayonnaise, beaten egg and a little salt and pepper to the potatoes and mix well until evenly combined and smooth. Fold in the flaked mackerel, parsley and 3 tablespoons of breadcrumbs and stir until evenly mixed and holding together nicely.

Tip the remaining breadcrumbs onto a sheet of baking paper or put onto baking sheet. Divide the fishcake mixture into four and shape into round patties about 10cm/4 inches in diameter. Coat both sides in the breadcrumbs, then roll to coat the edges. Chill until ready to cook.

Meanwhile, make the remoulade by grating the celeriac using a handheld grater or food processor with a grater disc. Mix the mustard, mayonnaise, lemon juice and a little salt and pepper together in a bowl, then stir in the grated celeriac. Spoon into a dish, cover and chill until needed.

To make the pickled vegetables, pour the vinegar and water into a saucepan, add the sugar, garlic, fennel seeds, thyme, dried chillies and salt and bring to the boil, stirring until the sugar has dissolved. Take off the heat and leave to cool. Put the mixed vegetables into

PICKLED VEGETABLES
100ml/3½fl oz white wine
   vinegar
300ml/½pt water
25g/1oz caster sugar
1 garlic clove, finely chopped
1 tsp fennel seeds
2 sprigs fresh thyme
¼ tsp dried crushed chillies
1 tsp fine salt
350g/12oz mixed vegetables
   to include diced carrots,
   shredded red cabbage, diced
   raw beetroot and diced
   dessert apple

a glass jar, pour over the vinegar mix, then press the vegetables beneath the surface of the vinegar. Cover and chill for at least 4 hours for the flavours to mingle. Kept in a airtight jar, the pickles should keep in the fridge for up to a week.

When ready to serve, preheat the oven to oven to 180°C/350°F/gas mark 4. Heat 2 tablespoons of the oil in a large frying pan, with a metal handle if you have one. Add the fish cakes and fry over a medium heat for 1–2 minutes on each side, turning until golden and adding extra oil if needed. Transfer the frying pan to the oven if the pan is ovenproof, or put the fish cakes on a baking sheet, and bake for 12–15 minutes until the fish cakes are piping hot in the centre.

Transfer to serving plates with spoonfuls of the celeriac remoulade and spoonfuls of the drained pickled vegetables.

COOK'S TIP Make use of the soft centres from any leftover baked potatoes or mash from the previous day.

If you haven't used fresh horseradish before, look out for it in the supermarket alongside the other root vegetables, it is similar in shape to a mouli radish with a coarser skin like a parsnip. Cut off the amount you need, peel, then finely grate.

Fish pie

Fish pie must be on the top ten list of comfort food dishes – packed with mixed fish, smoked mackerel, prawns and diced hard–boiled egg, this is a feast in a pie dish.

Serves 4
Prep 30 minutes
Cook 40–45 minutes

TOPPING
1kg/2¼lb potatoes, cut into
    chunks
25g/1oz butter
70g/2½oz cheddar cheese,
    grated
Salt and pepper

FILLING
500ml/18fl oz milk
1 onion, quartered
1 bay leaf
450g/1lb fish pie mix: ready
    diced salmon, white and
    smoked fish
25g/1oz butter
200g/7oz leeks, thinly sliced
3 tbsp cornflour
140g/5oz smoked mackerel
    fillets, skinned, broken into
    bite-sized pieces
70g/2½oz peeled cooked
    prawns, defrosted, rinsed
4 eggs, hard-boiled, peeled,
    chopped
15g/½oz fresh parsley, chopped

TO FINISH
25g/1oz pack lightly salted
    crisps, roughly crushed
55g/2oz cheddar cheese, grated

Add the potatoes to a saucepan of boiling water and simmer for 15–20 minutes until soft. Drain, leave to steam dry for a couple of minutes, then mash until smooth. Mix in the butter, cheese and salt and pepper. Cover and set aside.

Pour the milk into a deep frying pan, add the onion, bay leaf, fish pie mix and a little salt and pepper. Bring to the boil then turn off the heat, cover with a lid and set aside for 10 minutes. Strain the milk into a jug, recover the pan of fish and set aside.

Preheat the oven to 180°C/350°F/gas mark 4. Heat the butter in a saucepan, add the leeks and sauté over a medium heat for a few minutes until the leeks have just softened. Mix the cornflour to a paste in a small bowl with a little water, stir into the leeks, then gradually stir in the strained milk and bring to the boil, stirring continuously until thickened and smooth. Taste and adjust the seasoning.

Spoon the cooked fish mix into the sauce with any remaining milk, then add the smoked mackerel, prawns, chopped eggs and parsley. Gently mix together then spoon into the base of a 1.5ltr/2½pt pie dish. Spoon the mashed potato on top and spread into an even layer. Run a fork over the top, then sprinkle over the crushed crisps and remaining cheese.

Put the dish onto a baking sheet and bake for 35–40 minutes until the fish pie is piping hot and the topping is golden. Spoon onto plates and serve with buttered cabbage.

Beef pot pies

You can make and freeze these delicious individual pies before baking, for up to 6 weeks. Defrost overnight in the fridge and bake when you need them for a great after-work supper or after a day out visiting a National Trust place for a warming stomp through frosty grounds.

Serves 4
Prep 35 minutes
Cook 2 hours–2 hours
**   5 minutes**

1 tbsp vegetable oil
600g/1lb 5oz lean stewing
    steak, diced
300g/10½oz onions, diced
2 garlic cloves, finely chopped
3 sticks celery, diced
450ml/¾pt beef stock
100ml/3½floz red wine
2 bay leaves
2 sprigs fresh thyme
Salt and pepper
15g/½oz butter
115g/4oz mushrooms,
    quartered
4 tsp cornflour
200g/7oz carrots, cut into
    small batons

PASTRY
225g/8oz plain flour
Pinch salt
½ tsp dried mixed herbs
115g/4oz butter, diced
50g/1¾oz cheddar cheese,
    grated
1 egg beaten, plus extra beaten
    egg to glaze

Preheat the oven to 160°C/325°F/gas mark 3. Heat the oil in a large flameproof casserole, add the beef, a few pieces at a time until all the meat is in the casserole, then fry over a high heat for 5 minutes, stirring until evenly browned. Mix in the onions, garlic and celery and fry over a medium heat for 5 minutes until just beginning to colour.

Mix in the stock, red wine, bay leaves, thyme and a little salt and pepper. Bring to the boil, then cover and transfer the casserole to the oven for 1½ hours.

Heat the butter in a small frying pan, add the mushrooms and fry for 4–5 minutes until golden. Mix the cornflour with a little water in a small bowl then stir into the beef casserole with the mushrooms and carrots. Recover and return casserole to the oven for a further 30 minutes. Switch the oven off and leave to the casserole to cool.

Meanwhile, make the pastry. Add the flour to a large bowl or food processor with a little salt, the dried herbs and butter then rub the butter in with fingertips or pulse in processor until fine crumbs. Mix in the cheese and beaten egg with a teaspoon or two of water to make a smooth dough. Wrap in clingfilm and chill until beef is cooled.

Preheat oven to 190°C/375°F/Gas mark 5. Divide the beef mixture between four individual 250ml/8fl oz pie dishes, discarding the bay and thyme stems. Cut the pastry into four pieces and roll out one piece until a little larger than the top of the pie dish. Brush the dish edge with a little water then press pastry lid on dish. Trim off excess pastry then crimp the edge and make leaves from the trimmings. Brush with beaten egg and bake for 20–25 minutes until piping hot and pastry is golden. Serve with roasted Brussels sprouts with lemon and thyme and braised red cabbage.

Venison stew

Belton House, Lincolnshire, is renowned for its deer and supplies the café with award-winning venison from the estate. Diced venison can be found in your local butchers and even your local supermarket – if you haven't tried venison before, it is very lean and, as the deer are free to roam, is ethically farmed too.

Serves 4
Prep 20 minutes
Cook 2 hours 3 minutes–
2 hours 34 minutes

2 tbsp vegetable oil
350g/12oz diced venison
250g/9oz carrot, cut into
    2cm/¾ inch cubes
200g/7oz swede, cut into
    2cm/¾ inch cubes
100g/3½oz celery, cut into
    2cm/¾ inch cubes
250g/9oz onion, roughly
    chopped
2 garlic cloves, finely chopped
3 rashers smoked streaky
    bacon, diced
1 tbsp redcurrant jelly
5 juniper berries, roughly
    crushed
1 bay leaf
2 sprigs fresh rosemary
100ml/3½fl oz red wine
450ml/¾pt beef stock
Salt and pepper
20g/¾oz butter
115g/4oz mushrooms,
    quartered
2 tbsp cornflour

Preheat the oven to 180°C/350°F/gas mark 4. Heat half the oil in a large frying pan, add the venison and fry over a high heat for 5 minutes, stirring until evenly browned. Scoop out of the pan with a draining spoon and transfer to a casserole dish, then add the carrot, swede and celery to the venison.

Add the remaining oil to the frying pan and fry the onions, garlic and bacon over a medium heat, for about 10 minutes, stirring from time to time until the onions are golden and the bacon cooked.

Add the redcurrant jelly, juniper berries, bay leaf and rosemary to the onions, then pour in the wine and stock. Season with a little salt and pepper and bring to the boil. Pour over the venison, cover with a lid or foil and cook in the oven for 1½–2 hours or until the venison is tender.

Heat the butter in a frying pan, add the mushrooms and fry for 3–4 minutes until golden. Mix the cornflour with a little water in a cup to a smooth paste. Stir the mushrooms and cornflour into the casserole and return to the oven for 15 minutes. Spoon onto plates, discarding the bay and rosemary stems. Serve with creamy mashed potatoes flavoured with a little horseradish or chopped chives, or warm bread.

COOK'S TIP Venison is very lean with a strong gamey flavour, so you can use a little less than when cooking with stewing beef, especially when mixed with lots of winter vegetables. If you aren't a fan, you can substitute lamb neck fillet or lean stewing beef instead.

Chana masala

Lord Curzon of Kedleston Hall, Derbyshire, was Viceroy of India and based in the south of the country where this typical chickpea curry originates. The chefs at Kedleston developed this great vegan main course after hearing that more and more of the café customers were requesting meat-free dishes.

Serves 4–6
Prep 25 minutes
Cook 1 hour 35 minutes

2 x 400g/14oz cans chickpeas

COCONUT PASTE
100g/3½oz fresh coconut
    pieces
50g/1¾oz cashew nuts
1 tsp fennel seeds
½ tsp poppy seeds

WHOLE GARAM MASALA
3–4 cloves
2.5cm/1 inch piece cinnamon
    stick
1 cardamom pod, crushed
1 bay leaf
1 star anise

CURRY SAUCE
2 tbsp vegetable oil
340g/12oz onion, quartered
3 green chillies, halved,
    deseeded
2.5cm/1 inch piece root ginger,
    peeled, grated
3 garlic cloves, finely chopped
300g/10½oz or 3 tomatoes
Salt to taste

Drain and rinse the chickpeas, add to a saucepan, cover with fresh water and bring to the boil. Simmer for 1¼–1½ hours until tender.

Finely chop all the ingredients for the coconut paste in a food processor, then gradually blend in a little water to make a paste. Scoop into a bowl and reserve.

To make the curry sauce, heat the oil in a medium saucepan, add the whole garam masala ingredients and cook over a medium heat for 2–3 minutes to release the flavour.

Finely chop the onion and green chilli in the food processor, add to the pan and cook, stirring for about 5 minutes until softened and transparent. Add the grated ginger and chopped garlic and fry until it loses its raw smell, for about 5 minutes.

Chop 100g/3½oz or 1 tomato and purée the rest in the food processor. Stir the chopped tomato into the onion mix with a little salt, and cook until softened. Stir in the puréed tomatoes, and cook for 2–3 minutes.

Stir in all the dry spices. Pour in two thirds of the water, mix together and simmer for 5 minutes. Add the coconut paste and the remaining water and cook for 5 minutes, stirring from time to time.

Drain and add the cooked chickpeas to the pan and simmer for 5 minutes or until the sauce has thickened.

Continued overleaf

1 tsp chilli powder
¼ tsp turmeric
2 tsp ground coriander
450ml/16 fl oz water

TO FINISH
1 tbsp fresh chopped
    coriander, plus a little extra
    to garnish
¼ tsp ground garam masala
Salt to taste
1 tsp fresh lemon juice,
    optional

Sprinkle the chopped coriander and ground garam masala over the top, mix together and season to taste with salt and lemon juice, if using. Garnish with extra chopped coriander and serve with poori or pilau rice.

COOK'S TIP This recipe is also great using dried chickpeas that have been rehydrated. If you have a pressure cooker you can greatly reduce the cooking time of the chickpeas by adding soaked chickpeas and measured fresh water to the base of the pressure cooker – check the manual for amounts of water and cooking timings.

Banoffee cake

To meet the increasing demand for dishes in the café that suit specific dietary needs we have come up with this gooey, caramel-drizzled banana cake. It is dairy-free, egg-free and gluten-free and is a huge hit with our customers. For home-cooks, it means that you can just bake one cake and everyone can enjoy it together without anyone feeling that they have to have the separate option.

Cuts into 10–12 slices
Prep 30 minutes
Cook 58–64 minutes

300g/10½oz cooking apples, peeled, cored, diced
2 tbsp water
Oil for greasing
300g/10½oz dairy-free or soft margarine
225g/8oz soft light brown sugar
5 small bananas, total weight 500g/1lb 2oz with skins on
285g/10oz gluten free self-raising flour
2 tsp bicarbonate of soda
2 tsp ground mixed spice

TOPPING
100g/3½oz caster sugar
2 tbsp water
100ml/3½fl oz coconut milk

Add the cooking apples and water to a saucepan, cover and cook over a low heat for 10 minutes until soft, then leave to cool.

Preheat the oven to 160°C/325°F/gas mark 3. Lightly oil a 23cm/9 inch springform tin and line the base with a circle of non-stick baking paper.

Melt 50g/1¾oz of the margarine in a frying pan, add 70g/2½oz of the brown sugar and heat until the sugar has dissolved. Slice two of the bananas, add to the frying pan and cook until lightly coloured. Spoon in an even layer over the base of the springform tin.

Add the cooled apples and the remaining peeled bananas to the bowl of your food processor and pulse for a couple of seconds. Add the remaining margarine and sugar and pulse until the mixture is smooth and lump-free.

Spoon in the flour, bicarbonate of soda and mixed spice and pulse again. Scrape down the sides of the bowl and pulse again. Spoon the cake mixture over the bananas in the tin and smooth gently with a spatula into an even layer.

Bake for about 45–50 minutes or until well risen, golden brown and slightly cracked on top and a skewer inserted into the centre of the cake comes out cleanly. Leave to cool.

Loosen the edge of the cake with a knife, invert onto a serving plate, and remove the tin and lining paper.

Add the sugar to the cleaned frying pan with the water and cook over a medium heat until the sugar has dissolved. Tilt the pan to encourage the last grains of sugar to dissolve, then continue to cook for 3–4 minutes until the syrup has become a golden caramel. Take the pan off the heat, pour in the coconut milk and stand well back as it will bubble vigorously. Stir until smooth, then leave to cool for about 5–10 minutes until thickened slightly.

Pour the coconut caramel over the top of the cake, covering the bananas and drizzling down the sides a little. Leave to cool, then cut into slices.

COOK'S TIP Whenever making recipes for friends or family on a special diet always make sure to read the labels on the food packs carefully. Not all margarine is dairy-free – double check that there isn't any buttermilk or other hidden dairy products.

The cake mixture will look a little curdled, this is normal and doesn't affect the quality of the cake.

Chocolate & beetroot cake

This is a real crowd pleaser. Decorate with candles for a birthday cake, sparklers for a bonfire party or add festive decorations for an alternative to a traditional Christmas cake. Mixing beetroot purée into the sponge keeps it moist, while a little of the juice adds a pretty pink tinge to the frosting.

Cuts into 10 slices
Prep 40 minutes
Cook 1¼–1½ hours

375g/13oz fresh trimmed
   beetroot, scrubbed, roughly
   chopped
3 tbsp water, optional
5 eggs
250ml/9fl oz vegetable oil
250g/9oz caster sugar
225g/8oz self-raising flour
100g/3½oz cocoa
1 tsp baking powder

FROSTING
70g/2½oz butter, at room
   temperature
85g/3oz full fat cream cheese
250g/9oz icing sugar
dark chocolate shavings,
   optional

Preheat the oven to 160°C/325°F/gas mark 3. Line the base and sides of a 23cm/9 inch springform tin with non-stick baking paper. Add the beetroot to a food processor and blitz for 30–60 seconds to a smooth purée, adding the water if needed. Spoon into a sieve set over a bowl and leave for a few minutes to drain.

Spoon the beetroot purée back into the food processor or a mixer bowl, reserving the beetroot juice for the frosting. Add the eggs, oil and sugar, then the flour, cocoa and baking powder and blend until smooth.

Spoon the cake mixture into the lined tin and spread level. Bake in the oven for 1¼–1½ hours or until a skewer inserted into the centre of the cake comes out cleanly. If the cake appears to be browning too quickly, cover the top loosely with foil after 45 minutes.

Stand the cake tin on a wire rack and leave to cool in the tin.

For the frosting, beat the butter and cream cheese together until soft and smooth. Gradually beat in the icing sugar with 1–2 teaspoonfuls of the reserved beetroot juice to give a pale pink colour.

Remove the cake from the tin and peel away the lining paper. Put the cake on a serving plate, spread the frosting over the top and sprinkle with the chocolate shavings if using.

Sticky gingerbread

Rich, dark and very treacly, this super-spiced gingerbread almost tastes better a day or two after making. Slice and add to lunchboxes or pack with a flask of hot coffee when out hiking across one of our cliff-top walks or country estates.

Cuts into 10 slices
Prep 40 minutes
Cook 1 hour

225g/8oz plain wholemeal flour
3 tsp ground ginger
2 tsp ground mixed spice
1 tsp bicarbonate of soda
50g/1¾oz brown sugar
100g/3½oz butter or soft margarine
175g/6oz black treacle
50g/1¾oz golden syrup
1 tsp caraway seeds
150ml/¼pt milk
2 eggs

TOPPING
½ orange, juice and zest cut away from white membrane and cut into thin strips
½ lemon, juice and zest cut away from white membrane and cut into thin strips
50g/2oz caster sugar
25g/1oz root ginger, peeled, cut into thin strips

Preheat the oven to 160°C/325°F/gas mark 3. Line the base and sides of a 900g/2lb loaf tin with non-stick baking paper.

Add the flour, ginger, mixed spice, bicarbonate of soda and sugar to a bowl and stir together.

Heat the butter or margarine, treacle and golden syrup together in a saucepan over a low heat, stirring until the butter or margarine has melted. Remove the pan from the heat and stir in the caraway seeds and milk, then leave to cool.

Add the eggs to the cooled treacle mix and whisk together until smooth. Pour the liquid into the dry ingredients and whisk again until smooth. Pour into the lined tin and bake for about 45 minutes or until well risen and a skewer comes out cleanly when inserted into the centre of the cake. Leave to cool in the tin for 15 minutes.

Meanwhile, make the topping. Add the orange and lemon juice to a small saucepan with the sugar and bring to the boil, stirring until the sugar has dissolved. Add the fruit rinds and sliced ginger, and simmer gently for 15 minutes until just softening and the liquid has become syrupy.

Remove the cake from the tin, peel off the lining paper, then stand on a plate and spoon over the ginger, citrus zest strips and syrup and leave to cool completely. Cut into thick slices to serve.

COOK'S TIP Make sure the liquid mixture is cooled before you whisk in the eggs and when adding to the dry ingredients.

This cake freezes well without the topping. Wrap in fresh baking paper and foil, label and freeze for up to 6 weeks.

Mincemeat tea cakes

Estate agents often say the smell of homemade bread sells houses – well, the smell of these gently spiced teacakes just says Christmas is on the way.

Makes 8
Prep 30 minutes
Rising 1½ hours
Cook 12–15 minutes

250g/9oz strong plain flour,
    plus extra for dusting
125g/4½oz plain flour
30g/1oz caster sugar
2 tsp easy blend dried yeast
120ml/4fl oz milk, lightly
    warmed
3–6 tbsp warm water
½ tsp salt
50g/1¾oz butter, at room
    temperature, cut into pieces
Little oil for greasing
1 tsp ground cinnamon
1½ tsp dried mixed spice
125g/4½oz fruit mincemeat

TO GLAZE
15g/½oz butter
2 tsp honey

Place the flours, sugar, yeast, milk, 3 tablespoons water and salt in the bowl of your mixer and beat with a dough hook until the dough forms and pulls away from the sides of the bowl, adding a little more warm water if needed.

Gradually add the butter, and continue to mix on a low speed until smooth. Alternatively, beat the ingredients in a bowl with a wooden spoon, then knead the butter into the dough on a chopping board, or straight onto the work surface.

Put the dough into a clean bowl, cover the top with oiled clingfilm and leave in a warm place to rise for about 1 hour, until doubled in size.

Tip the dough out onto a lightly floured work surface and stretch into a rectangle. Mix the cinnamon and mixed spice into the mincemeat then spoon the mincemeat over the centre of the dough. Fold the dough over the mincemeat to cover. Dust the dough with a little flour, then knead until the mincemeat is fully incorporated.

Cut the dough in to eight even-sized pieces, roll each piece into a round, then put onto a baking sheet lined with non-stick baking paper, leaving space between the teacakes to rise. Cover loosely with oiled clingfilm and leave in a warm place for about 30 minutes, until doubled in size. Preheat the oven to 200°C/400°F/ gas mark 6.

Remove the clingfilm from the teacakes and bake for 12–15 minutes until well risen and golden in colour. Tap the bottoms and they will sound hollow when done.

To make the glaze, gently heat the butter and honey together in a small pan until the butter has melted. Brush over the warm teacakes and leave to cool. Serve split and buttered.

Cherry Bakewell custard cake

This magical topsy-turvy gluten-free cake is quite unlike any other cake. As it cooks it will separate into three layers: a bottom layer of sponge, topped with a layer of custard, with a thinner layer of fluffier sponge, then fruit on top.

Cuts into 10–12 slices
Prep 30 minutes
Cook 1 hour 5 minutes–
   1 hour 10 minutes

Little oil for greasing
200g/7oz cherry pie filling
4 eggs, separated
150g/5½oz caster sugar
3 tsp vanilla extract
125g/4½oz butter or soft
   margarine, melted
115g/4oz gluten free self-
   raising flour
500ml/18fl oz milk, warmed

Preheat the oven to 180°C/350°F/gas mark 4. Lightly oil a 23cm/9 inch springform tin and line the base with a circle of non-stick baking paper. Make sure it is tightly clipped together and wrap the outside of the tin with foil. Spoon the cherry pie filling into the bottom of the tin.

Add the egg yolks to the bowl of your mixer with the sugar and vanilla and whisk with a balloon whisk until light and fluffy.

Whisk the egg whites in a second bowl with a clean dry balloon whisk until stiff peak stage.

Slowly trickle the melted butter or margarine into the egg and sugar mixture, whisking continuously. Add the flour and whisk until just combined. Gradually whisk in the milk until smooth.

Gently whisk one third of the egg whites into the egg yolk mixture. Fold in the remaining egg whites and mix gently, don't worry if there are a few lumps. Pour into the tin over the cherry pie mix.

Bake for 1 hour 5 minutes–1 hour 10 minutes until the cake is well risen with a slight wobble when the tin is tapped. Leave to cool on a wire rack. Chill in the fridge for 1 hour, or longer if you have time, then loosen the edge of the cake with a knife. Cover the tin with a large plate and then invert the cake onto the plate and remove the tin and lining paper. Cut into wedges to serve.

COOK'S TIP The cake will sink down a little as it cools so don't be alarmed the first time that you make this.

Not all supermarkets sell canned pie filling, so if you can't find it then you can use 100g/3½oz defrosted frozen pitted cherries.

Rice pudding brûlée

Rice pudding is one of those old school desserts that never goes out of fashion. Here it is has been given a festive twist by spooning over a spiced dried fruit and apple compote, then finishing with a crisp brittle caramelised sugar topping.

Serves 6
Prep 20 minutes
Cook 1 hour

700ml/25fl oz milk
140g/5oz pudding rice
55g/2oz caster sugar
1½ tsp vanilla extract
4 tbsp double cream

FRUIT COMPOTE
50g/1¾ oz ready-to-eat dried
 apricots, diced
50g/1¾ oz stoned dates, diced
1 small dessert apple, peeled,
 quartered, cored, diced
1 small orange, grated zest
 and juice
½ tsp ground cinnamon
¼ tsp ground nutmeg
Pinch ground cloves
1 tbsp maple syrup

TOPPING
6 tsp demerara sugar

Preheat the oven to 150°C/300°F/gas mark 2. Pour the milk into a saucepan, bring to the boil then stir in the rice, sugar and vanilla extract. Pour into a casserole dish, cover and cook in the oven for about 1 hour or until the rice is tender. Stir, then set aside to cool and thicken.

Meanwhile, make the fruit compote by adding the apricots, dates and apple to a small saucepan. Stir in the orange zest and juice then the spices and syrup. Bring to the boil then cook gently for 15–20 minutes until the fruit is soft. Set aside.

When ready to serve, divide the fruit between the bases of six individual heatproof ramekin dishes. Stir the cream through the cooled rice, then spoon over the fruit and spread level. Sprinkle the top with the demerara sugar, then caramelise with a cook's blowtorch or by cooking the dishes until the grill. Leave to cool for 5 minutes, then serve while the sugar topping is crisp and brittle.

Chestnut, rum & chocolate pavlova cake

This impressive layered meringue dessert was create by the team at Sizergh in Cumbria, who were inspired by the story of the sweet chestnuts in their grounds. After a visit to Versailles, Cecilia Strickland returned with sweet chestnut seeds, which she planted at her home at Sizergh. These splendid trees, although ancient now, can still be seen today. For a modern labour-saving version, do use a can of sweetened chestnuts rather than peeling and puréeing the chestnuts from scratch.

Serves 10–12
Prep 40 minutes
Cook 1½ hours

6 large egg whites
340g/12oz caster sugar
2 tsp vanilla extract
600ml/1pt double cream
200g/7oz dark chocolate,
   broken into pieces
2 x 250g/9oz cans sweetened
   chestnut purée
2 tbsp dark rum
Dark chocolate shavings,
   optional
Little sifted cocoa to decorate

Preheat the oven to 110°C/225°F/gas mark ¼. Line three baking sheets with non-stick baking paper and draw a 20cm/8 inch circle onto each, using a cake tin as a template.

Add the egg whites to a large bowl and whisk with an electric mixer until stiff peaks and the bowl can be turned upside down without the egg whites moving. Continue whisking and gradually whisk in the sugar, a tablespoonful at a time, until all the sugar has all been added. Whisk for a minute or two more until very thick and glossy, then gradually whisk in the vanilla.

Divide the meringue equally between the lined baking sheets, spreading into three flat circles within the marked lines.

Bake for 1½ hours or until the paper can be peeled easily away from the base of the meringue circles. Turn off the oven and leave the meringues in the oven to cool completely.

Pour 400ml/14fl oz cream into a saucepan and slowly bring to the boil. Remove from the heat, add the chocolate and stir until melted and smooth. Leave to cool in the fridge until thick enough to spread.

Mix the chestnut purée and rum in a second medium-sized bowl. Whip the remaining cream in a third bowl until it forms soft swirls, then fold into the chestnut mix.

To serve, take one of the meringue discs off the baking paper and put onto a serving plate with the flat underside uppermost. Gently spoon over one third of the chocolate cream and spread into an even layer, followed by a layer of the chestnut mix. Repeat with the second meringue, chocolate cream and chestnut cream, then top with the remaining meringue with the swirly top-side uppermost. Spoon over the remaining chocolate cream, spread into an even layer, then spoon the chestnut cream a little in from the edge so that there is a band of chocolate cream showing.

Decorate with a few chocolate shavings, if using, and dust with a little sifted cocoa. Chill in the fridge until ready to serve.

COOK'S TIP The meringues can be made the day before, kept on their baking paper, covered with clean tea cloths and put in a cool dry place or leave in the oven but make sure no one in the family turns it on!

Lemon drizzle cake

Everyone loves a lemon drizzle cake but this one is a little different. Not only does it use gluten-free flour, but also mashed potato for added moistness, with all the tanginess that you would expect from a good lemon cake.

Cuts into 12 slices
Prep 30 minutes
Cook 1 hour

CAKE
Little oil for greasing
250g/9oz dairy-free margarine
  or butter
250g/9oz caster sugar
370g/13oz cooked, cooled
  mashed potato
5 eggs
1 lemon, grated zest only
½ tsp gluten-free baking
  powder
225g/8oz self-raising gluten-
  free flour

TOPPING
115g/4oz icing sugar, sifted
1 lemon, grated zest and
  2 tbsp juice

Preheat the oven to 150°C/300°F/gas mark 2. Lightly brush the inside of a 23cm/9 inch springform tin with a little oil and line the base with a circle of non-stick baking paper.

Cream the margarine or butter and sugar together in a mixer until light and fluffy and the mixture doesn't feel gritty.

Add the cooled mashed potato, eggs, lemon zest, baking powder and gluten-free flour. Beat until smooth, scraping down the sides of the bowl and making sure there is no dry flour left on the bottom of the bowl.

Spoon into the tin, level the top, then bake for about 1 hour until well risen, golden brown, the top is slightly cracked and a skewer comes out cleanly when inserted into the centre of the cake.

Add the icing sugar to a bowl, gradually stir in enough lemon juice to make a thin smooth glacé icing, then mix in half the lemon zest. Run a knife around the edge of the cake, remove the springclip side then lift off the base with a palette knife and peel away the lining paper. Put onto a wire rack set over a large plate. Drizzle the icing over the top of the hot cake, sprinkle with the remaining lemon zest and leave to cool.

Transfer to a serving plate and cut into slices to serve.

COOK'S TIP At the café in Fountains Abbey, North Yorkshire, we scoop the potato out of leftover baked potatoes for this recipe, a really good way of using them up, although it does give a sponge cake with a slightly closer texture.

Make sure that the mixture is beaten very well and don't worry if it looks split, this is due to the potato and the flour and is normal.

Conversion charts

WEIGHTS

7.5g	¼ oz	450g	1lb
15g	½ oz	500g	1lb 2oz
20g	¾ oz	565g	1¼ lb
30g	1oz	680g	1½ lb
35g	1¼ oz	700g	1lb 9oz
40g	1½ oz	750g	1lb 10oz
50g	1¾ oz	800g	1¾ lb
55g	2oz	900g	2lb
60g	2¼ oz	1kg	2lb 3oz
70g	2½ oz	1.1kg	2lb 7oz
80g	2¾ oz	1.4kg	3lb
85g	3oz	1.5kg	3½ lb
90g	3¼ oz	1.8kg	4lb
100g	3½ oz	2kg	4½ lb
115g	4oz	2.3kg	5lb
125g	4½ oz	2.7kg	6lb
140g	5oz	3.1kg	7lb
150g	5½ oz	3.6kg	8lb
170g	6oz	4.5kg	10lb
185g	6½ oz		
200g	7oz		
225g	8oz		
250g	9oz		
285g	10oz		
300g	10½ oz		
310g	11oz		
340g	12oz		
370g	13oz		
400g	14oz		
425g	15oz		

All eggs are medium unless stated
otherwise. Use either metric or imperial
measures, not a mixture of the two.

VOLUME

5ml	1 teaspoon	
10ml	1 dessertspoon	
15ml	1 tablespoon	
30ml	1fl oz	
40ml	1½ fl oz	
55ml	2fl oz	
70ml	2½ fl oz	
85ml	3fl oz	
100ml	3½ fl oz	
120ml	4fl oz	
130ml	4½ fl oz	
150ml	5fl oz	
170ml	6fl oz	
185ml	6½ fl oz	
200ml	7fl oz	
225ml	8fl oz	
250ml	9fl oz	
270ml	9½ fl oz	
285ml	10fl oz	½ pint
300ml	10½ fl oz	
345ml	12fl oz	
400ml	14fl oz	
425ml	15fl oz	¾ pint
450ml	16fl oz	
465ml	16½ fl oz	
500ml	18fl oz	
565ml	20fl oz	1 pint
700ml	25fl oz	1¼ pints
750ml	26fl oz	
850ml	30fl oz	1½ pints
1 litre	35fl oz	1¾ pints
1.2 litres	38½ fl oz	2 pints
1.5 litres	53fl oz	2½ pints
2 litres	70fl oz	3½ pints

LENGTH

5mm	¼ in
1cm	½ in
2cm	¾ in
2.5cm	1in
6cm	2½ in
7cm	2¾ in
7.5cm	3in
9cm	3½ in
10cm	4in
18cm	7in
20cm	8in
22cm	8½ in
23cm	9in
25cm	10in
28cm	11in
30cm	12in
35cm	14in
38cm	15in

Oven temperatures

DESCRIPTION	FAN	CONVENTIONAL	GAS
Very cool	100°C	110°C/225°F	Gas ¼
Very cool	120°C	130°C/250°F	Gas ½
Cool	130°C	140°C/275°F	Gas 1
Slow	140°C	150°C/300°F	Gas 2
Moderately slow	150°C	160°C/320°F	Gas 3
Moderately slow	160°C	170°C/325°F	Gas 3
Moderate	170°C	180°C/350°F	Gas 4
Moderately hot	180°C	190°C/375°F	Gas 5
Hot	190°C	200°C/400°F	Gas 6
Very hot	200°C	220°C/425°F	Gas 7
Very hot	220°C	230°C/450°F	Gas 8
Hottest	230°C	240°C/475°F	Gas 9

Picture Credits

p6 Clive Goudercourt, Development Chef.
© National Trust Images/William Shaw.

p12 Weights resting on weighing scales in the
window bay in the Kitchen at Plas yn Rhiw, Pwllheli,
Gwynedd. © National Trust Images/Robert Morris.

p13 Blossom in May at Acorn Bank, near Penrith,
Cumbria. © National Trust Images/Paul Harris.

p56 Copper kettles and brass draining spoons and
ladles in the Great Kitchen at Saltram, Devon.
© National Trust Images/John Hammond.

p57 Flowers growing in the walled garden at Ickworth,
Suffolk. © National Trust Images/Justin Minns.

p100 Wooden butter shapers on the quarry tiled floor
of the Living Room at Rosedene, Worcestershire.
© National Trust Images/Robert Morris.

p101 Trees and fern in a forest in autumn on Brownsea
Island, Dorset. © National Trust/Chris Lacey.

p148 Detail of lead-lined sink with earthenware bowls
and early nineteenth-century cutlery in 1840s Back to
Backs house, Birmingham. © National Trust Images/
Dennis Gilbert.

p149 Frost on vegetation on the riverbank of the Wey
Navigations at Send, Surrey. © National Trust Images/
Derek Croucher.

All other images by Nassima Rothacker.

Index